7-nt

[new title in England]

Jesus the Radical, rev. ed.
(London : IVP, 1989

I Came to Set the Earth on Fire

R. T. France

A PORTRAIT OF JESUS

InterVarsity Press
Downers Grove
Illinois 60515

InterVarsity Press is the book publishing
division of Inter-Varsity Christian Fellowship,
a student movement active on campus
at hundreds of universities, colleges and
schools of nursing. For information about
local and regional activities, write IVCF,
233 Langdon St., Madison, WI 53703.

New Testament quotations are generally taken
from *Today's English Version* (TEV), published
by the American Bible Society in 1966
under the title *Good News for Modern Man*.
I have occasionally used other versions, or
supplied my own, where TEV seemed
inappropriate.

References to the Gospels use the abbreviations
Mt. (Matthew), Mk. (Mark), Lk. (Luke) and
Jn. (John). Names of other biblical books are
given in full. Where parallel passages occur in
two or more Gospels only one reference is
normally given. Those interested in comparing
the parallel accounts should use a Synopsis
of the Gospels, or follow the marginal
references in a Reference Bible.

Cover art: Antoni Clave's *Descent from the
Cross*, courtesy of the Cincinnati Art Museum.

ISBN 0-87784-642-1
Library of Congress Catalog
Card Number: 75-32128

Printed in the United States of America

Contents

Preface

If the description is not too presumptuous, this book is an attempt to write a modern 'Gospel'.[1] It is a book about Jesus, aiming to show his significance not only to the people of his own day, but to us as well, but doing this by studying the historical facts of his life. I have not attempted a systematic presentation of his teaching, though inevitably a good deal of his teaching has come in along the way. But what I have tried to do is to look at the records of his life, and to assess how he would have appeared to those who met him, not only in a brief encounter, but as his constant companions and disciples. What they could have seen and understood of his mission, and what some of them have recorded for us of the impression he made on them, must surely be the starting-point for any realistic assessment of the significance of Jesus for us today.

So I have made no attempt here to unravel the question of who Jesus was, the paradoxical combination of the human and the divine which has teased the minds of Christians and their critics from the first century until now. The Gospels provide the raw materials for an answer

[1] See below, pp. 180–190, for a discussion of the nature of the four Gospels and their value as sources for a study of Jesus.

to that question, and indeed they themselves begin the process of answering it; John in particular goes a long way along the road.[1] It is a question which everyone who studies the life of Jesus must answer for himself, and it is my hope that this book will spur its readers towards discovering their own answer. But to discuss that question would need another book.[2]

No doubt many readers will complain that my account of Jesus is incomplete, perhaps that it is one-sided. Their favourite emphases, favourite incidents, even perhaps their favourite problems and objections, are ignored, or passed over too lightly. But this is inevitable. Any portrait of Jesus is bound to be selective; there is far more to Jesus than will compress into a single paperback! And the selection must equally inevitably be personal, and must reflect the beliefs and interests of the writer.

It has always been so. It was on this rock that the 'lives of Jesus' which were popular in the nineteenth century so often came to grief. The idea was to produce an objective, unbiased account of Jesus' life. But always the writer's own background and ideas governed the presentation, and so we had the liberal Jesus, the pacifist Jesus, Jesus the prophet of doom, and many other Jesuses to suit the climate of their times.

I do not imagine for a moment that I have escaped from a similarly one-sided approach. I do not think anyone can escape it. But then I do not want to. You cannot describe Jesus dispassionately. Even if you could succeed in doing so, the result would be an impossibility, a clinically non-theological Jesus who could never have inspired the devotion of millions and founded the world's greatest religion. Those who try to be objective about Jesus have missed the point. For Jesus does not allow objectivity. He demands decision.

[1] See especially Jn. 1:1–18.   [2] See below, p.177, note 3.

1 Nazareth

'Can anything good come from Nazareth?' asked Nathanael.

'Come and see,' replied Philip, and took him to meet Jesus.

And Nathanael, for all his scepticism, was impressed by this unknown preacher from rustic Nazareth. In fact he became one of his most devoted followers.[1]

That is the sort of thing that happens when Jesus is around. People find their prejudices shaken. Some of them respond by digging themselves deeper into their trenches. Others find themselves, to their amazement, abandoning the preconceptions of a lifetime, and they are never the same again.

Nathanael had good reason to be sceptical. Not only was Nazareth in Galilee, which made it half-pagan in the eyes of a good Jew of Jerusalem. Even for a Galilean like Nathanael, who came from Cana, only eight miles away, it was of no importance – a little country town in the hills, scarcely more than a village, with no historical associations, no claim to fame, overshadowed by the neighbouring

[1] Jn. 1:45–49.

Galilean capital, Sepphoris. For Philip to claim that the long-expected deliverer of the Jews had appeared in Nazareth was ludicrous. It was also practically blasphemous, because every good Jew knew that the deliverer would be a descendant of the great king David, and would come from the very correctly Jewish town of Bethlehem, David's home, a mere two hours' walk from Jerusalem. Nazareth indeed!

So Jesus, the carpenter from Nazareth, had no easy task to convince his Jewish compatriots that he was the one sent by God to deliver them. But if it was an uphill task in Jerusalem, surely in his own Galilee he would find a hearing more readily. Surely Nazareth above all would jump at the honour of being the home-town of the national deliverer, and he could expect to be sent on his mission with full civic honours.

Nazareth decides

In Nazareth, therefore, Jesus staked his claim, and he did it in the synagogue. Every Sabbath day the community would gather in the synagogue for a session of teaching and worship. The books of the law and the prophets were read, and the contents explained by one of the leading citizens. A notable visitor could expect to be invited to say a few words. So the synagogue was the natural platform for any man with a message.

Jesus, fresh from his first preaching tour, returned to Nazareth, and attended the synagogue.[1] His fame was already spreading, so an invitation to teach was automatic.

He was given the book of Isaiah the prophet. He would be expected to read a short passage, and then comment on its significance, and that was just what he did. He read from chapter 61:

[1] The following account is based on Lk. 4:14–30.

'The Spirit of the Lord is upon me.
He has anointed me to preach the Good News to the poor,
He has sent me to proclaim liberty to the captives,
And recovery of sight to the blind,
To set free the oppressed,
To announce the year when the Lord will save his
    people!'

Did he choose the passage himself, or was it the set reading for the day? It is hard to say. Scholars are not agreed whether the readings from the prophets were fixed at this period. Even if they were, Jesus was seldom one to be bound by traditional rules, and it would be very much in character for him to substitute a more directly relevant reading for the one set. At any rate, whether set or not, the passage was a very significant one. It describes the work of God's 'anointed one'. It was one of many Old Testament passages in which the Jews of that time found a description of the work of the Messiah ('anointed one'), the deliverer whom God was going to send to his people, and whom they were eagerly expecting.

There was a pregnant pause. 'All the people in the synagogue had their eyes fixed on him,' says Luke. No doubt some of them guessed what was coming.

'Then he began to speak to them: "This passage of scripture has come true today, as you heard it being read."' There it is, simple, clear, unmistakable – and breathtaking. The carpenter is claiming to be the Messiah. Jesus is the fulfilment of the hopes of centuries. The great day has come. And it has come, of all places, in Nazareth.

No doubt he said much more, which Luke has not seen fit to record. But those few words are quite enough to show the audacity of Jesus' claim. Yet he must have put it very persuasively, because the first reaction Luke records is a favourable one: 'They were all well impressed with him, and marvelled at the beautiful words that he spoke.' So far Jesus has the audience on his side.

But then they began to think of the implications. 'Isn't he the son of Joseph?' Who is he to make such claims? We have known him since he was a child. He isn't even a properly trained Rabbi. Can we take him seriously? Where is the proof of his claim?

And that led on to other thoughts. They had heard of his remarkable success as a healer. Here was a possible line of proof; yet he had healed no-one in Nazareth. It was all hearsay. If Nazareth was to produce the Messiah, surely it could at least expect a generous share of his miraculous activities. Jesus put it into words for them: 'I am sure that you will quote the proverb to me, "Doctor, heal yourself." You will also say to me, "Do here in your own home town the same things we were told happened in Capernaum." ' And he went on to ruin irrevocably the good impression he had made by pointing out that God's prophets had never shown favouritism to their own people, and that he had no intention of breaking the pattern. His words must have been as uncompromising as they had been attractive before: 'All the people in the synagogue were filled with anger when they heard this. They rose up, dragged Jesus out of town, and took him to the top of the hill on which their town was built, to throw him over the cliff. But he walked through the middle of the crowd and went his way.' As far as we know, he never came back.

Whatever Jesus was, he was not ordinary. He provoked extreme reactions, whether of acceptance or of rejection. One moment they were all on his side, the next they were trying to lynch him. And yet such was the authority of this extraordinary man that apparently he simply walked through a murderous crowd, and nobody laid a finger on him.

Division

That is how Luke introduces his account of the mission of Jesus. It is not only a dramatic story in its own right; it is also typical of Jesus' ministry, and of the way people reacted to him. He met enthusiastic acceptance, and bitter hostility, for it was hard to be neutral about Jesus. He drove people to extremes, and in so doing he divided them, deeply and irrevocably, into two opposing camps. 'Anyone who is not for me, is really against me', he said; and conversely he told his followers that 'whoever is not against you is for you'.[1] But there does not seem to be much room for neutral spectators.

Jesus was not in the habit of mincing his words. Sometimes he deliberately exaggerated to make his meaning unmistakable, as in this remarkable pronouncement: 'Do not think that I have come to bring peace to the world; no, I did not come to bring peace, but a sword. I came to set sons against their fathers, daughters against their mothers, daughters-in-law against their mothers-in-law; a man's worst enemies will be the members of his own family.'[2] Exaggerated? Perhaps, though family persecution is still the experience of many followers of Jesus, as it has always been. At any rate, Jesus' point is clear enough. He is a divider, a disturber of the peace. People's reactions to him cause some of the deepest divisions this world knows. If you understand Jesus, you can't be neutral about him.

This is the Jesus of the Gospels, the only Jesus history can recover. Many other Jesuses have been invented. The liberal theologians of the last century invented a sentimental Jesus who was all for peace and harmony and social justice, the great preacher of the fatherhood of God and the brotherhood of men. The modern humanist invents a Jesus who is the supreme example of self-giving service to

[1] Lk. 11:23; 9:50.   [2] Mt. 10:34–36.

13

his fellow-men. Many of us have been brought up on an anaemic Jesus, friend of little children, incapable of any angry thought or divisive action.

All these Jesuses contain some genuine features, of course. Jesus did preach the virtues of love and forgiveness; he did attack exploitation and injustice; he is the supreme example of self-sacrifice for others; he did encourage little children to come to him, and recommend the childlike attitude. The Jesus who said, 'Come to me, all of you who are tired from carrying your heavy loads, and I will give you rest'[1] is a wonderful reality. But we gain nothing by suppressing the other, sterner aspect of the Jesus of the Gospels, the Jesus men were prepared to kill, and to die for, the Jesus who was sufficiently dynamic and controversial to start the most lasting revolution the world has seen.

Jesus today

It is the failure of Christians to present this aspect of Jesus to the world that has made it possible for so many today to adopt an attitude of neutrality, or more often of complete indifference. The world has seen plenty of high-minded reformers, plenty of gentle philanthropists, plenty of altruistic social workers. Long may they continue. But if Jesus is no more than one of that noble army, he merits no more than the nod of retrospective appreciation which he receives from many people today.

Yet still today there are those who find in Jesus much more than that, an object of fanatical devotion, or of equally fanatical hatred. The 'Jesus Movement' is one recent example of this which has caught the public imagination, hordes of young people whose commitment to Jesus and his cause is unmistakably absolute, however defective

[1] Mt. 11:28.

their theology may sometimes be; and they are only the newsworthy fringe of a vastly greater number of enthusiastic young devotees, who may lack the panache of the 'Jesus Movement', but who are no less deeply committed. On the other side the Communist governments use every weapon they can find to stamp out the followers of Jesus, and the measures taken by Jewish, Islamic and Buddhist national governments show that they are seriously worried by Christian activity, while the small band of vocal humanists in Britain show by their hysterical tirades that Jesus is still a real threat. Those who understand who Jesus is and what he stands for are still today driven to extreme reactions.

It is only those who do not understand who can be indifferent, and dismiss Jesus with a well-meant but patronizing word of praise. And there are still a lot of them. It is for them particularly that I have written this book, to try to show why Jesus provokes so much enthusiasm and so much hatred. A book of this size must necessarily be selective.[1] But I have tried to present enough of the Jesus we meet in the Gospels to explain why people wanted to kill him, and to die for him, and why even today people's attitudes can be no less extreme.

I want to try to do justice to the Jesus who said, 'I came to set the earth on fire.'[2]

---

[1] See the Appendix (p. 180) for a statement of the principles on which the book has been written.
[2] Lk. 12:49.

2 Expectation

Not long after Jesus was born, his parents presented him in the temple at Jerusalem, as the law required. An old man met them there, and took the baby in his arms, with a strange poetical prayer which has been famous ever since:

'Now, Lord, you have kept your promise,
And you may let your servant go in peace.
For with my own eyes I have seen your salvation,
Which you have made ready in the presence of all peoples;
A light to reveal your way to the Gentiles,
And to give glory to your people Israel.'[1]

He was called Simeon, and hardly anything is known about him, except that he 'was a good and God-fearing man, and was waiting for Israel to be saved'.[2] As such he was typical of many Jews of his time. But Simeon was convinced that he would see the fulfilment of his hopes before he died. And now, in this baby in the temple, he was sure it had come: Israel would be saved.

Jesus was a Jew, and he spent his life among Jews. If we are to understand him, we must know something of what it

[1] Lk. 2:29–32.   [2] Lk. 2:25.

meant to be a Jew in the first century AD, the harsh realities of political subjection to an imperial power, the hopes and the fears of those who called themselves the people of God, the ideology which motivated a man like Simeon.

Political subjection

For more than 700 years the Jews had been a subject people, more or less, ever since King Ahaz took the fateful step of inviting the imperialist power of Assyria to protect him against his threatening neighbours. The nation was too small to be independent in a world of competing empires. Often they had changed hands: the Assyrians, the Egyptians, the Babylonians, the Persians, the Greeks, and the Hellenistic empire of Syria had ruled them in turn, until that famous interlude when Syrian oppression had become just too much, and Judas Maccabaeus had led them to independence again by a remarkable guerrilla campaign which must surely be the envy of many twentieth-century freedom fighters. For a century they had been independent, in theory at least. But all the time in the background there was Rome, without whose goodwill that independence would have proved fragile. Rome could afford to wait, as her power and influence increased. Meanwhile, the glorious independence of the Maccabees degenerated into a chaos of intrigues and opposing factions, until in 63 BC the Roman general Pompey, called in by a deputation of Jews to put an end to their rulers' quarrels, captured Jerusalem. Thus Jewish independence, such as it was, was lost, never to be recovered for two thousand years. Lost, but not forgotten. The exploits of Judas Maccabaeus lived on as an inspiration for those who could not accept a subject status for the people of God.

The Romans were not yet ready for direct rule. It suited them better to instal local princelings who would dance to their tune. The most famous of these was Herod 'the Great', at the end of whose long and extravagant reign Jesus was born. Herod owed his position to Rome, and his loyalty was made conspicuous by the foundation of cities named in honour of the emperor, and temples for his worship. But to the Jews he was a tyrant, and a foreigner. He was, in fact, from the related Idumaean tribe, but he was not a true Jew, and his marriage to a Jewish princess (among several other wives!) was not sufficient to win his people's favour. Outwardly he supported the Jewish religion, and his magnificent new gold and ivory temple at Jerusalem was one of the wonders of the world, but like many magnificently extravagant rulers he was harsh and oppressive.

When Herod died in 4 BC, the Jews petitioned Rome for a change of government. But Rome had no complaints about Herodian rule, and so confirmed Herod's will which divided the country into three smaller states ruled by three of his sons. Archelaus, who took over the most important division consisting of Judaea and Samaria, centred on Jerusalem, proved a disastrous failure, and was deposed ten years later. Here the Romans for the first time imposed direct rule, incorporating Judaea into the province of Syria, under its own local governor (a Roman). Herod Antipas, who received the area of Galilee with some territory east of the Jordan, survived longer than his brother. He governed Galilee ('ruled' would be to exaggerate his status; the Romans refused to call him 'king') throughout the period of Jesus' life, and is the Herod with whom both John the Baptist and Jesus were involved. Philip, a half-brother of Archelaus and Antipas, governed the more remote area of Ituraea and Trachonitis to the north-east, and has no direct bearing on the story of Jesus.

So the effective governors in Palestine at the time of

Jesus' activity are Herod Antipas, the unpopular half-Jewish[1] governor of Galilee, the area of Jesus' upbringing and early activity, and Pontius Pilatus, the Roman prefect of Judaea from AD 26 to 36, a man known chiefly to the world as the weakling who gave in to Jewish pressure and had Jesus killed, but attested to in non-Christian sources of the period as a harsh, brutal, and perhaps rather stupid governor, with a hearty racial contempt for his subjects, the typical District Officer of British colonial tradition.[2]

Pilate was not a good representative of his government's policy. Rome always tried to respect Jewish scruples and to protect their strange religion. Anti-Jewish prejudice was rife in popular Roman thought; it was a natural product of the total lack of comprehension on both sides. But the government saw the value of toleration. It was forbidden to carry the imperial standards (regarded by the Jews as idolatrous) in Jerusalem, or to provoke Jewish religious resistance in other ways. But Rome was far away, and Pilate (and he was not alone in this) enjoyed stirring up their impotent fury.

Economic grievances

To the psychological and ideological irritant of Roman rule must be added the much more practical grievance of Roman economic policy. The Jews had their own temple tax and other religious dues to pay, but the *pax Romana* was not a free gift either. There were dues on land and cattle, duties on trade and transport of goods, but above all a considerable poll-tax, rigorously enforced through periodic censuses, which was a perennial cause of unrest.

[1] His father was Idumaean and his mother Samaritan, both related to the Jews, but both totally rejected by them.
[2] For further details on Pilate see below, pp. 149–154.

It has been calculated that the total taxation, Jewish and Roman together, may have exceeded 40% of an ordinary man's income.

An elaborate taxation system demands an elaborate civil service, and it was here that the grievances were multiplied. The lucrative privilege of tax-collection went to the highest bidder, who then farmed the work out to smaller fry, and they in turn to others. The top men would be Romans; the lower ranks, who actually made contact with the people, were Jews. And each had to make his position profitable to himself. Provided the correct tax was produced, the officials would not worry about how it was collected. So the officially required tax was swollen by the necessary rake-off at each level of the civil service, and the name 'tax-collector' became in common parlance a synonym for an unscrupulous quisling and extortioner. If there were honest tax-collectors, they were rare exceptions. When tax-collectors asked John the Baptist how they should show their repentance, he replied, 'Don't collect more than is legal.'[1] That alone would be a sufficiently striking break with the normal pattern to show their genuineness.

The Jewish establishment

In any occupied country there will always be those who resist, and those who collaborate, as well as the vast mass of people who just go on existing regardless. The collaborators in Roman Palestine included not only those who used the Roman occupation as a road to easy money, but also those who owed their political and religious influence to the favour of Rome. Ever since the days of the Maccabees religious and political leadership had been joined in the same hands, and under the Romans the leading priests were still the highest political authority in Judaea under the

[1] Lk. 3:12, 13.

governor. The Sanhedrin, under the chairmanship of the High Priest, was both the supreme religious council and the national parliament. It was also the supreme court for all except political charges. Their powers were limited by Roman rule, but their influence was still enormous. To the ordinary Jew, they were the true government.

But they owed their position to Rome. The prefect could, and did, appoint and depose High Priests at will. In a politically explosive situation their tenure was far from secure, and much depended on keeping the country quiet. A threat to this equilibrium, such as Jesus came to represent, could expect little sympathy in these quarters.

The dominant party in this ruling élite were the Sadducees.[1] Conservative in their religious traditions, they nevertheless exhibited the ability, still shared by too many religious conservatives, to acquiesce in a political and social *status quo* which many of their more sensitive compatriots could not accept. They were an aristocratic minority, more concerned with maintaining the traditions of temple worship, and their own political influence, than with the hopes and fears of ordinary men. If they, like Simeon, were 'waiting for Israel to be saved', they had too much diplomatic tact to show it. Probably they were well satisfied with things as they were.

Hopes of God's intervention

But most Jews were far from satisfied. Ever since the spectacular empire of David and Solomon had broken up, and Israel and Judah had lapsed into third-rate powers, or less, the people of God had come increasingly to believe that the God who had chosen them had something better

[1] See, however, below, pp. 92, note 2 and 93, note 2, on the complexities of the Jewish 'parties'. The account here is necessarily a drastic over-simplification.

planned for them. King after king fell short of their hopes, and eventually both kingdoms were shattered, and Judah survived only as a province of an eastern empire. But all this only caused the hope of God's ultimate intervention to grow. The 'day of the Lord' must come soon, and it would see Israel restored to her true place at the head of the nations. Lyrical poems looked forward to that day as a new exodus, a new creation even, when peace and harmony would flourish, and God and man be reconciled. But always at the centre of these pious hopes stood Israel, the chosen people of God.

While many of the Old Testament prophets spoke simply of God himself visiting and saving his people, as time went on more and more prophecies included another figure, a man through whom God would carry out his work of salvation. The Old Testament does not use the word 'Messiah' (God's 'anointed') with this meaning, but in the centuries before the Romans came this term gained ground, and by the time of Jesus it would be readily understood in this sense. Its Greek version was 'Christ'.

There is no such thing as *the* Jewish Messianic hope. Many quite independent ideas are usually grouped under this term. Some looked for a new and greater prophet, some for a priestly leader, some for a supernatural figure, a sort of angelic judge. But the dominant hope was for a king like David, and that meant, by the time of Jesus, a warrior capable of defying the power of Rome and restoring the political glory of Israel. The theologians may have had other ideas, but if you had spoken to the man in the street about the 'Messiah', he would certainly have understood you to mean the 'son of David', the warrior king of the coming empire of Israel.

Hopes of political deliverance were taken further in a new type of book known as 'apocalypse'. Several of these have survived, written by Jews in the period around the first centuries BC and AD. Here the coming deliverance from Rome is taken up into a cosmic battle between good and evil, presented in vivid imagery and extravagant symbolism. Always the conviction is that the climax is imminent, and the reign of the powers of evil (often only thinly disguised) is about to be broken. Then God and his people will reign for ever. These were more than morale-boosting broadsheets. They embodied a vital conviction, which grew stronger in many Jews as the period of Roman power lengthened, that things were fundamentally wrong in the world, and only a catastrophic intervention by God could put them right.

Political activists

Simeon, we have seen, was 'waiting for Israel to be saved', and so were large numbers of his compatriots. But some were not prepared to wait. Pious hopes were not enough. God helps those who help themselves. The situation was ripe for insurrection.

In AD 6, the year when Judaea was brought under a Roman governor, and a census was ordered to provide the figures for taxation, a revolt broke out under the leadership of Judas of Galilee, who denounced paying taxes to Rome as disloyalty to God, the true ruler of Israel. His revolt came to nothing; but his action provided the inspiration for a new breed of freedom fighters whose uncompromising opposition to foreign rule led eventually to the catastrophic Jewish War of AD 66–70, in which Jerusalem was totally destroyed. Prominent in this war were the Zealots, whose name is often used, inaccurately but conveniently, to cover the whole activist movement.[1]

[1] 'Zealot' as a party designation probably did not come into use until the outbreak of war in AD 66. Before that, several different groups of

Many of the activist leaders who appeared after Judas came from Galilee, so that the word 'Galilean' took on the political overtone of 'revolutionary'. These leaders were sometimes known as 'prophets', and if they were not explicitly hailed as 'Messiah' by their followers, it cannot have been far below the surface. And Jesus was a crowd-puller from Galilee! A man who announced himself as the fulfilment of Old Testament hope, and that in Galilee, was involved in an atmosphere of revolution, whether he liked it or not.

Scribes and Pharisees

The chief colleague of Judas of Galilee in the revolt of AD 6 was a certain 'Zadok the Pharisee'. The image of a Pharisee in most modern thought is of a pedantic stickler for ritual details, a crusty academic with little time for the existential concerns of ordinary men. For a Pharisee to be in the fore-front of a guerrilla movement seems incongruously worldly. But that is because we have successfully stowed our religion in a separate compartment from the rest of life, and expect the first-century Jew to do likewise. In fact Zadok was in the true line of succession from the fore-runners of the Pharisaic movement. These were men who had fought beside Judas Maccabaeus to preserve their freedom to practise their religion as the Law demanded, in the face of Antiochus' determined attempt to replace traditional Judaism with the worship of the Greek gods. Since those days Pharisaism had, of course, tended to fossilize, and Jesus' strictures on the unfeeling legalism of

---

activists had emerged, frequently in conflict with each other, some essentially religious, with 'prophetic' leaders, others primarily political, like the Sicarii ('dagger-men') mentioned in Acts 21:38. To call them all 'Zealots' is like describing all Britons as 'Cockneys'! But it has become standard practice, and a book like this is not the place to be pedantic. I shall use 'Zealot' in this wide and inaccurate sense.

the Pharisees of his day seem to have been well deserved. But their fanatical loyalty to the Law of God made it impossible for them, like the Sadducees, to be happy under Roman rule, and made them, at least potentially, allies of the Zealots.

Whether it led them to war or to study, the Pharisees' primary loyalty was to the Law, not only the Law of Moses, but the already considerable later elaborations of the basic Old Testament Law, which were to grow over the next few centuries to the enormous bulk of the Babylonian Talmud, which fills a good-sized library shelf by itself! The aim was to legislate for every part of life, and there were few human activities whose correct performance was not laid down in meticulous detail.[1] The tortuous debates for which Rabbinic Judaism is famous had already begun, and there was already a distinct class of men, the 'scribes', whose job it was to know and interpret and to elaborate further the legal material. Most of the scribes were drawn from among the Pharisees.

The Pharisees could not perhaps be called popular, but they commanded considerably more respect from ordinary people than did the aristocratic Sadducees. By and large they were sincere, if one-sided, in their teaching and practice. But they suffered from the common complaint of those whose chief aim in life is to be more conspicuously holy than the next man, a profound disdain for the man in the street. The verdict on the Jerusalem crowd attributed to the Pharisaic leaders by John leaves an unpleasant taste: 'This crowd does not know the Law of Moses, so they are under God's curse!'[2]

Religious separatists

At least the Pharisees kept in the main stream of life, and

---

[1] See below, pp. 96, 97, for some examples.   [2] Jn. 7:49.

did not withdraw altogether from contact with ordinary folk. There were some who felt this step was necessary. The discovery during the last thirty years of several complete scrolls and a mass of fragments from caves near the Dead Sea has brought to light a Jewish monastic community of the period of Jesus, who found in this inhospitable region an ideal retreat from contact with their fellow-men. In violent opposition to the Jerusalem temple authorities, they saw themselves alone as the Sons of Light, the true people of God. They studied the Old Testament avidly to find predictions relating to themselves, and showed marvellous ingenuity in making every phrase apply to their own present situation. Their study had led them to the conviction that the final confrontation between light and darkness, between God and evil, was near, and they kept themselves in constant readiness for the coming war, in which they would infallibly triumph over all the Sons of Darkness.

This Qumran sect was virtually unknown to historians until the chance find of an Arab shepherd started a train of discoveries; there may well have been other such groups in this barren area, which has always attracted the ascetic and the separatist.

The revival of prophecy

It was in this same area of the Jordan valley and the rocky desert which flanks the western shore of the Dead Sea that a solitary preacher began to attract attention, some thirty years after the death of Herod the Great. The date was, probably, AD 28.[1] The man was John, son of a Jeru-

---

[1] Luke's very careful dating (3:1) unfortunately still leaves some room for uncertainty, as it has been argued that the years of Tiberius' reign may have been calculated not from AD 14, the year of Augustus' death, but from the beginning of his co-regency with his father some two years earlier.

salem priest, who had left his home for an ascetic life in this desert area. Some have argued that he joined the Qumran community. Certainly, as a religious ascetic in the same area, he must have had contact with them, and possibly with other such groups. But by the time he came to the notice of the public he was not the emissary of any particular sect, but a solitary 'voice', owing allegiance to God alone, and with a message which, in all its essentials, has no parallel at Qumran. If he can be compared to anyone else, it is to the Old Testament prophets, particularly the rough-hewn Elijah, on whom indeed he seems to have modelled his ascetic style of life and his distinctive camel-hair clothes. It was many generations since prophecy had fallen out of use in Israel; but now once again a prophet was announcing imminent judgment as fiercely as any Amos or Joel, and calling the people of God to repentance.

The most obvious innovation in John's preaching, from which he derived his nickname, was his insistence that those who accepted his call to repentance should be baptized in the Jordan. A visible token of response has been a favourite demand of preachers through the ages, but John's was no mere call for a show of hands. Baptism was a requirement for converts to the Jewish religion. Yet John was demanding that *Jews* should submit to it. The Jewish crowds who came to hear him were denounced as 'snakes' trying to escape from the fire of God's anger,[1] and to make matters quite plain John said that there was no point in their appealing to their descent from Abraham, since 'God can take these rocks and make descendants for Abraham!'[2]

So John's baptism amounted virtually to a recognition that to belong to Israel was no automatic guarantee of God's favour, a message which we have already seen

[1] Lk. 3:7.
[2] Lk. 3:8, a telling pun on the very similar Aramaic words for 'rocks' and 'children'.

embodied in Jesus' manifesto at Nazareth, and which we shall meet again. Despite his impressively staged prophetic image, John was as far as possible from the Zealot type. He had not come to herald the glory of Israel, but her destruction, if she would not repent.

The amazing thing is that he was so popular. The crowds came from miles around, and the inevitable speculation that he might be the Messiah seems to have died hard. But John claimed no status for himself except that of a forerunner, and insisted that the Messiah was soon to come, indeed that he was already there. Not that he used the word 'Messiah', apparently; but he talked about one greater than himself who was going to baptize not with water but 'with the Holy Spirit and fire', and who was ready to gather up his grain and burn the chaff, a judge and a divider of men.

Not a very appealing message, we might think. But John was obviously in earnest, and the 'Baptist' movement caught on, preparing for the judgment of God, the coming of the 'greater one'. There was no ready-made congregation down there by the Jordan apart from a few ascetics and other dropouts; but the strangest assortment of people gathered to John's call, from tax-collectors to, amazingly, Pharisees and even Sadducees (thought these last may have been there more for surveillance than for repentance!). The Jordan valley became a rallying-point for many who were 'waiting for Israel to be saved'.

How long the movement lasted we do not know, for the very good reason that our main sources[1] are not interested

[1] These 'main sources' are Mt. 3:1–12; Mk. 1:1–8 and Lk. 3:1–20, together with the account of John's death in Mk. 6:14–29. Jn. 1:19–37; 3:22–30 adds further details. The Jewish historian Josephus (*Ant.* xviii. 5. 2 (116–119)) confirms the general picture, though he does not mention any connection with Christian origins, and presents John primarily as a moral reformer whose popularity made him, unjustly, suspect as a potential source of sedition.

in the 'Baptist' movement for itself, but only in so far as it gave rise to another greater movement. For the news of John's activity soon spread into the Galilean hills, and among those who joined the pilgrimage to the Jordan was a relative of John from those parts, Jesus of Nazareth.

3 Preparation

A certain Galilean once went about enquiring, 'Who has *'amar* ?' 'Foolish Galilean,' they said to him, 'do you mean an "ass" for riding, "wine" to drink, "wool" for clothing or a "lamb" for killing ?'[1]

This Jewish joke, which pokes fun at the slovenly speech of Galilee with its indistinct vowels and dropped aitches, indicates the Jerusalem Jew's attitude to his northern neighbours. Galilee had once been predominantly Gentile territory, and even now its population was far from completely Jewish. Cut off from Judaea by the hostile territory of Samaria, and under a different system of government, it tended to develop along its own independent lines of speech and character, and of religious tradition. Hence the great disdain in which a Judaean Jew held his Galilean brother.

It was from Galilee that Jesus came. His friend Peter was immediately recognizable in Jerusalem by his northern accent,[2] and the evidence suggests that Jesus too would have spoken a strongly 'Galilean' Aramaic. His home at Nazareth was, as we have seen, barely on the map of Jewish affairs at all, and it is remarkable that Jesus' recorded

[1] Babylonian Talmud, *'Erubin* 53b.   [2] Mt. 26:73.

activity in Galilee is entirely confined to the less significant small towns like Capernaum, Cana and Nain, and bypasses the prosperous centres of provincial life like Sepphoris and Tiberias. Respected as Jesus undoubtedly was among his own people, in the eyes of Jerusalem he was a backwoodsman.

His family was probably what we would call 'middle-class'. The carpenter was a skilled craftsman, perhaps employing labour, and certainly an important figure in the village economy. But they were not wealthy: the offering of two turtle-doves made after the birth of Jesus[1] was a concession allowed to those who could not afford a lamb,[2] and several of Jesus' parables reflect the circumstances of a very ordinary home.[3] Fine clothes were only for those who lived in palaces.[4]

The birth of Jesus

Jesus was born into such a family about 6 BC. It is impossible to be sure about the date, beyond saying that the traditional dating on which the years of the Christian era are based is certainly wrong! Jesus was born before the death of Herod the Great in 4 BC, probably not very long before that date.[5]

[1] Lk.2:24.   [2] Leviticus 12:8.
[3] E.g. Lk. 11:5-7; 15:8-10.   [4] Lk. 7:25.
[5] He was 'about thirty' (Lk. 3:23) when he was baptized by John, whose activity began, as we have seen, about AD 28. Luke's connection of Jesus' birth with a Roman census under Quirinius (Lk. 2:1, 2) does not settle the question, as no census is otherwise attested in the period of Herod's rule; indeed it seems politically rather unlikely; and Quirinius is not known to have been governor of Syria at that time, though he is known to have been posted there at a later date (AD 6), when he was responsible for the census which provoked Judas' revolt. The arguments are too complex to be pursued here. A vigorous, though disputed, vindication of Luke's data is given by E. Stauffer, *Jesus and His Story* (ET, SCM Press, 1960), pp. 27-36. P. W. Barnett, *Expository Times* 85 (1973/4), pp. 377-380, suggests that the 'enrollment' was not a tax census at all, but a formal listing of citizens who were required to take the oath of allegiance known to have been administered by Herod about 7 BC. For a brief summary of the argu-

The story of Jesus' birth at Bethlehem needs no telling: it is probably the best-known story in the whole Bible. But it is worth remembering that it was at Bethlehem, in Judaea, that Jesus was born, away from home, in what was probably unfamiliar, even slightly hostile, territory, despite Joseph's Judaean ancestry. Indeed, their failure to find a proper place to stay even at such a crucial time as a first childbirth may be due not only to the overcrowding of the little town with census officials and with others brought there like Joseph for registration, but also in part to the Judaean attitude to Galileans. If the Rabbis could compare marrying an uneducated girl to lying with a beast,[1] it may not have seemed out of place to allow a Galilean girl to have her baby in a stable!

Of course, it may have been a blessing in disguise. No-one is sure what the 'inn' was like, whether it was a guest-room in a private house, or a typical eastern *khan* where all comers slept where they could find room in a large open courtyard. If it was the latter, the stable may well have proved a lot quieter and more private, and the manger more comfortable than the courtyard floor.

Whatever the precise situation, Jesus was born in an alien environment, in circumstances which in twentieth-century Britain would surely spark off a press campaign for the homeless, if not a question in Parliament. A strange beginning for 'great David's greater Son'!

'Born of a virgin'

It all sounds very ordinary. Yet Christians speak about the

---

ments see L. Morris, *St Luke* (Tyndale New Testament Commentary, Inter-Varsity Press, 1974), pp. 81–83, and for a fuller discussion, based on a Ph.D. dissertation, D. J. Hayles, *Buried History* 9 (1973), pp. 113–132; 10 (1974), pp. 16–31; Hayles concludes in favour of Luke's reliability.
[1] Babylonian Talmud, *Pesaḥim* 49b.

birth of Jesus as something quite out of the ordinary. They talk about the 'Virgin Birth'. That is not an everyday occurrence!

First let it be said that 'Virgin Birth' is a misnomer. There is no suggestion of anything physiologically abnormal about the *birth* of Jesus: it is his *conception* which is in question. Matthew and Luke, in quite different ways, state clearly that Jesus was not, biologically, the son of Joseph, but that Mary conceived without human intercourse, by the power of God. Joseph and Mary were engaged, but not yet married, at the time, and Joseph was shocked to discover that she was pregnant.[1]

Such a story lends itself to misunderstanding, and jokes about Jesus' father being a Roman soldier billeted in Nazareth have been current since at least the middle of the second century.[2] Others, less offensively, assume that Joseph was in fact the father, and explain the 'mistake' of Luke and Matthew by the loose use of the word 'virgin' to refer to one who has not yet had a child,[3] or regard the story as an imaginative creation from Isaiah 7:14, which Matthew in fact quotes in this connection.

Some such explanation must, of course, be found if the possibility of a miraculous birth is ruled out *a priori*. Like the great miracle at the other end of Jesus' life, the resurrection, it is unparalleled, and therefore, to modern secular thought, impossible. We shall have to look more fully at miracles later.[4] Whether you can accept them depends not primarily on the evidence, but on your view of the limits of possibility. The evidence for the bodily resurrection of Jesus could hardly be stronger, but that does not prevent

[1] See Mt. 1:18–25; Lk. 1:26–38.
[2] Origen, *Contra Celsum* i. 32, *etc.* The story is a commonplace in early Jewish polemic against the Christians.
[3] So G. Vermes, *Jesus the Jew* (Collins, 1973), pp. 218–222.
[4] See below, pp. 73–76, and on the resurrection, pp. 169–170.

many people refusing to believe it.

In the case of the virgin birth, the evidence is not so complete: Mark and John do not mention it, explicitly at least, and the rest of the New Testament shows no clear knowledge of it. But as far as it goes it is quite unambiguous. Either you write off Matthew and Luke as uncritically credulous story-tellers, or worse (and Luke's reputation as a careful historian is in fact deservedly high[1]), or you make allowance as they did for a world in which God is active and miracles can happen. The story of Jesus belongs in such a world, and a miraculous birth is not out of place at the beginning of such a story. Not that the Christian understanding of Jesus as 'Son of God' stands or falls by this tradition: the New Testament writers came to this belief on other grounds. But the man who cannot accommodate a birth without a human father within his understanding of what God can do is going to make heavy weather of much of the story of Jesus, indeed of the Christian faith.

The hidden years

Back home in Nazareth, Jesus was brought up in, for us, almost total obscurity. His later teaching shows that he had a full and sound grasp of the Hebrew Scriptures, but that is no more than any pupil of the village synagogue-school could gain if he took his opportunity seriously. The level of literacy and formal education among the Jews was probably as high as in any other part of the Roman Empire, and a good grounding in the Old Testament Scriptures was the primary goal of this education. The one story of Jesus' childhood preserved by Luke shows him avidly pursuing this education, and amazing the Jerusalem pundits by his progress. To find such eagerness and intelligence in a Galilean boy was no doubt particularly surprising.[2]

[1] See below, pp. 184, 185.   [2] Lk. 2:42–50.

34

But Jesus had no opportunity for higher education such as his later follower Saul of Tarsus enjoyed in the Pharisaic 'university' of Jerusalem. It seems likely that Joseph died while Jesus was young. (That, at least, is the common deduction from his failure to appear alongside Mary in the Gospel stories, and from the fact that Jesus was known in Nazareth as 'Mary's son'.[1]) This would leave Jesus, as the eldest son, with a considerable responsibility as the male head of the family, and probably manager of the family business. With at least four younger brothers and an unknown number of sisters to be brought up,[2] the hope of formal education beyond the normal level must have been remote. At least Jesus, for all his remarkable grasp of the Old Testament, could not compete in paper qualifications with the scribes. To the superior eyes of Jerusalem he was uneducated.[3]

Yet it is from this long 'hidden' period of Jesus' life that many of the most effective features of his later teaching are no doubt derived. Most of Jesus' parables focus on the experiences and events of life in a village setting: several are set on the farm or in the vineyard; others draw on the daily pattern of life in a village house, or that great excitement in village life, a wedding; one shows us the children playing in the market-place, another the shepherd out on the hills, another the fishermen by the lake. They include many unforgettable, and often light-hearted, portraits of people (drawn perhaps from well-known local characters?): the shrewd but unscrupulous manager, the eccentric employer, the power-drunk local magistrate cut down to size by the nagging widow. One of the secrets of the appeal of Jesus' teaching to such a variety of cultures over so many centuries is its firm earthing in ordinary everyday life and in the unchanging features of human character. It is not

[1] Mk. 6:3. [2] *Ibid.* [3] Jn. 7:15.

difficult to recognize yourself, and your neighbours, in many of Jesus' parables. If he had grown up in the monastic isolation of Qumran or the academic remoteness of Jerusalem, his teaching might have been no more widely known than that of any other contemporary Rabbi or sectarian leader. The thirty years in Nazareth were put to good account.

Thirty years is a long time, half a lifetime. How far Jesus was aware for those thirty years that he was bound for a more significant work than that of the village carpenter, we cannot hope to know. No doubt he had heard something of the strange circumstances of his birth; no family could keep a secret like that, even if they wanted to. Our one glimpse into his childhood seems to show that even as a boy he was aware of a special relationship with God.[1] Once his mission was launched he showed a sense of urgency which drove him to Jerusalem against all the dictates of common-sense: 'I came to set the earth on fire, and how I wish it were already kindled! I have a baptism to receive, and how distressed I am until it is over!'[2] And yet, for those thirty years, he waited. It was not yet time.

The baptism of Jesus
Then came the news of the appearance of a new prophet down in the Jordan valley. The Gospels speak of John's crowds as being drawn from Judaea and the Jordan region, but news travels fast, and John's family was related to that of Jesus. We do not know whether others from Galilee went with him, but Jesus, perhaps already aware that this was the time he had been waiting for, was among those who presented themselves for baptism.

Matthew tells us that John was shocked, and 'tried to make him change his mind. "I ought to be baptized by

[1] Lk. 2:49.   [2] Lk. 12:49, 50.

you," John said, "yet you come to me!" [1] Many since then have been similarly perplexed as to why Jesus, whom Christians have always believed to have been not only John's spiritual superior, but in fact sinless, should have accepted a baptism which was explicitly a token of repentance and a plea for forgiveness. Jesus' reply to John's protest doesn't seem to give much help either: 'Let it be this way for now. For in this way we shall do all that God requires.' (Literally, 'thus it is fitting for us to fulfil all righteousness'.) How does it 'fulfil all righteousness' for Jesus to pose as a sinner if he was not?

It is always dangerous to try to penetrate the psychology of someone known to us only from the writings of others, particularly if that someone is unique; it would be a bold man who dared to think the sinless man's thoughts for him! Does being sinless demand, indeed does it allow, the *consciousness* of being sinless? To ask such a question explicitly shows its absurdity. A Jewish-Christian Gospel of, probably, the second century provides the *reductio ad absurdum* of this line of thought when it puts this into the mouth of Jesus: 'What sin have I committed, that I should go and be baptized by him? Unless perhaps this very thing I have just spoken is ignorance' (and therefore sinful!).[2]

Perhaps the most probable explanation is that Jesus' baptism had nothing to do with any personal consciousness of sin, but was a way of identifying himself with what John's movement stood for. John, as we have seen, was striking at the roots of the national self-confidence of the Jews. Jewish descent alone was worthless. Only those who mended their ways could hope to stand up to the coming judgment. Those who accepted John's baptism were declaring themselves for this new, purified Israel of God. As we shall see later, this idea of the true Israel as a body

[1] Mt. 3:14.   [2] Cited by Jerome, *Adversus Pelagianos* iii. 2.

37

depending not on nationality but on spiritual response was important in Jesus' teaching too, and Jesus' baptism must be seen, in part at least, as a 'vote' for this new spiritual community.

More than that, in identifying himself with those who were expressing in the Jordan their renunciation of sin, Jesus put himself in a position to be their representative. One day this identification was to drive him to death, and in that death he would die for them. Jesus' whole life, and his death, were 'for others', and his baptism was a declaration of this solidarity. How much of this was in his mind as he stepped into the Jordan it is impossible to say; but it is interesting that he was to use 'baptism' later as a symbol for his suffering and death.[1]

Whatever the motives which brought Jesus to the Jordan, his baptism in fact proved the occasion for much more than a declaration of his solidarity with repentant Israel. 'As soon as Jesus came up out of the water he saw heaven opening and the Spirit coming down on him like a dove. And a voice came from heaven: "You are my own dear Son. I am well pleased with you." '[2] Mark's account might suggest that this was a vision seen by Jesus alone, but the other Gospels in different ways indicate that it was intended as a witness to others as well. Indeed, John's Gospel makes it the moment of John the Baptist's conviction that Jesus was the one whose coming he had predicted.[3] At any rate, it was a deeply significant experience for Jesus himself, and from this point on he abandoned the humdrum life of Nazareth, and became for the rest of his life a wandering preacher, totally dedicated to his mission.

But what was that mission? We shall have to consider this question more fully later; but this vision which launched him on his course tells us a lot about it. The

[1] Mk. 10:38, 39; Lk. 12:50. [2] Mk. 1:10, 11. [3] Jn. 1:32–34.

38

coming of the Spirit of God[1] marked Jesus out as the Messiah. The passage which he chose as his manifesto at Nazareth opens with the same idea,[2] and several references in later Jewish literature show that this was a widespread element in Messianic expectation. The voice from heaven marked him out as Son of God, in a unique sense.[3] That Jesus was already conscious of such a relationship seems to be indicated by his remark about 'my Father's house' at the age of twelve, but this was something much more decisive. The words of the declaration echo two old Testament passages,[4] the first of which hails the Davidic king as the son of God, and the second introduces 'my servant', a figure in the book of Isaiah whose innocent suffering came to play a large part, as we shall see, in Jesus' understanding of his mission.[5] So the ten brief words of the voice at Jesus' baptism summed up the main lines of his mission as Messiah, Suffering Servant and, above all, Son of God.

The test

We have already been reminded of the danger of trying to pry into the psychology of Jesus on the basis of a few brief records. To say precisely what this experience at the Jordan meant to him in his understanding of himself and his mission would be rash. But that it was an experience of crucial importance is indicated not only by the fact that it set his life on a new course of public activity, but also by the immediate sequel as the Gospels record it. 'At once the

[1] The idea of a dove as a symbol for the Spirit was established in Jewish thought, on the basis of Genesis 1:2, with its description of the Spirit of God 'fluttering' over the waters at the creation. See Babylonian Talmud, *Ḥagigah* 15a.
[2] See above, pp. 10, 11.
[3] The Greek word represented by 'own dear' in the quotation from Mark above is frequently used in the Bible for an *only* Son.
[4] Psalm 2:7; Isaiah 42:1.
[5] See below, p. 118.

Spirit made him go into the desert. He was there forty days, and Satan tempted him.'[1]

Down there by the Jordan Jesus was in the region favoured by many then, as now, for getting away from ordinary life for a period of quiet thought and prayer. It is not surprising that he took the opportunity to work out the implications of what had happened. And it was in this process of coming to terms with who he was and what he had to do that he faced a decisive test: 'If you are God's Son, . . .'

After the voice of God came the voice of Satan.

Nowadays Satan gets a mixed reception. While most people, at least in the sophisticated atmosphere of Western materialism, deny his existence and laugh at medieval images of horns and hooves and toasting-forks, he is also acquiring an increasing number of devoted followers and practitioners of his arts. We shall have to look at this question of the demonic dimension later,[2] for this is by no means the only time it impinges on the story of Jesus. But here we get as close as we could hope, or wish, to the heart of the matter. For here we find Jesus alone with Satan. The story, if it is true at all, must have come from Jesus himself; there were no reporters present. So to Jesus at least Satan was no illusion, and his temptations were a force to be reckoned with.

The familiar list of three temptations given by Matthew and Luke[3] can be misleading if it is regarded as the sum total of the temptations Jesus ever faced. Luke in fact concludes his account with the remark that the Devil left Jesus alone 'for a while'. The Letter to the Hebrews insists that Jesus 'was tempted in every way that we are',[4] and the Gospels give us no reason to dispute that statement. But

[1] Mk. 1:12, 13.   [2] See below, pp. 70–72.
[3] Mt. 4:1–11; Lk. 4:1–13.   [4] Hebrews 4:15.

here in the desert near the Jordan Jesus faced the crucial test, the question of what he would make of his newly-confirmed position as Son of God. The three 'temptations' are not unconnected suggestions, but three ways of exploring what Jesus' mission entailed, and how the Son of God should relate to his Father.

It is this question of relationship that is all-important. Should he take it into his own hands to satisfy his hunger by his undoubted miraculous power, or trustfully accept this period of privation as his Father's will, designed for his spiritual profit? Should he force his Father's hand by artificially creating a crisis which demanded a miraculous rescue, or simply accept that his Father's help was real and available, without the need to test it? Should he take the easy way to the fulfilment of the Messianic goal which his Father had set before him, even at the expense of compromising his loyalty? The temptation was not to doubt his status or his destiny, but to misuse them. But for Jesus a relationship of obedience, trust, and absolute loyalty to his Father came first, and defeated the appeal of short cuts and cast-iron assurances. He proved to be truly the 'Son of God'.

This understanding of Jesus' desert experience is derived from the answers which he gave to the three suggestions. All are concerned with his relationship with God, not with his appeal to men. If there was also the temptation to achieve instant success by spectacular miracles or free food, Jesus' replies do not hint at it. It is his sonship which is under fire, not the methods to be adopted in his mission. Jesus himself, not his programme, is under the microscope.

His three replies to Satan were all drawn from the Old Testament. More remarkably, all three are drawn from the same short section of the book of Deuteronomy, chapters 6–8, a part of Moses' briefing of the Israelites before they crossed into the promised land. They had spent long years of hardship in the desert, and had faced tests of their loyalty to God which they had failed, and would fail again. Moses' words, spelling out what loyalty to God in such a time of testing involves, supply Jesus with his own guidelines as he too faces his testing in the desert. Israel, God's firstborn 'son',[1] had had its sonship severely tested, and had failed. Jesus faced the same tests and came through with flying colours, the true Son of God. We shall see later that Jesus saw himself as the true fulfilment of Israel's hopes and promises; it is not fanciful to see this conviction already spelt out in his replies to Satan.[2]

So the 'temptation' proved in fact the occasion for a further and more down-to-earth grasp of what Jesus' mission was going to involve. To be Messiah and Son of God was not going to be a formula for spectacular success, but for unquestioning trust and obedience, even when his Father's purpose led to a style of life and death which few Jews would have expected of the 'son of David'.

The mission begins

So Jesus was ready to launch his public mission. How exactly he did so we cannot be sure. While the first three Gospels seem to suggest that he immediately returned to Galilee, the Gospel of John records various early incidents in Judaea, and it seems most probable that these incidents, or some of them, came before Jesus' Galilean mission.[3]

---

[1] Deuteronomy 8:5; *cf.* Exodus 4:22.
[2] This understanding of the temptation story is more fully set out in my *Jesus and the Old Testament* (Tyndale Press, 1971), pp. 50–53.
[3] The events of Jn. 1:35 – 4:42 are not recorded in the other Gospels, and are explicitly dated before John's imprisonment (3:24), culminating in a deliberate 'retreat' to Galilee (4:1–3). The Galilean ministry with which the other Gospels begin is dated *after* John's imprisonment (Mk. 1:14).

At the centre of this early activity was a campaign of baptism, parallel to that of John, but separate from his, and apparently Jesus' baptism movement soon attracted greater numbers than John's.[1] John's followers regarded Jesus as a rival, though John apparently discountenanced this attitude. The Gospels testify, however, to a continuing difference, if not conflict, between the two, with John finding it difficult to perceive in Jesus' ministry the sort of fiery judgment he had predicted,[2] and Jesus himself pointing out the contrast between John's dour asceticism and his own free and easy attitude to fasting.[3] The two movements remained separate throughout the New Testament period,[4] and there are references to a sect of John's followers continuing as late as the third century AD in Syria. Some have even traced their descendants in the present-day Mandaeans of Iraq, but the Mandaeans' veneration of John is more likely derived second-hand from Christian tradition than by direct descent.

If Jesus first attracted attention as a second Baptist, this was clearly no more than a preliminary stage of his ministry, and there is no record of his administering baptism after these early days (though of course he laid down the practice for his followers to observe after his death). The event which seems to have led Jesus to change both his type of ministry and his location was John's imprisonment, attributed by the Gospels to his undiplomatic criticism of Herod Antipas' marriage,[5] and by Josephus to his excessive popularity, which made Herod suspect political sedition.[6] Both may well be true. The latter gives particular point to

[1] Jn. 3:22–30; 4:1, 2.   [2] Mt. 11:2–6.
[3] Mt. 11:18, 19: Mk. 2:18–20.
[4] See, e.g., Acts 18:24, 25; 19:1–5, and the frequent references in John's Gospel to the relations between John and Jesus, which suggest that there was still a significant Baptist movement to be considered when John wrote.
[5] Mk. 6:17, 18.   [6] Josephus, Ant. xviii. 5. 2 (116–119).

Jesus' 'tactical withdrawal' to a preaching ministry in Galilee: it was too early to court martyrdom by continuing a style of mission which had landed John in the castle of Machaerus, from which he never returned.

So, 'after John had been put in prison, Jesus went to Galilee and preached the Good News from God.'[1] This is the beginning of the phase of his mission which brought him to the preacher's seat in the synagogue at Nazareth, from which we began.

Additional note

The outline of Jesus' ministry

So far I have tried to deal with the few events recorded from the early life of Jesus in chronological order. But already we have begun to run into difficulties, and from this point on such difficulties increase. None of the Gospels is intended to be simply a chronicle of events in the order in which they occurred, and there are significant variations in the order in which they relate the same events. I have discussed this, and other matters of critical study of the Gospels, in the Appendix[2] rather than take up valuable space in the body of the book.

From this point on, therefore, I intend to discuss the activity of Jesus by themes, rather than make any pretence of chronological order. Many words could be wasted over chronological matters, and they would leave us little closer to our object of understanding the Jesus of the Gospels. Only when they come to the last week of Jesus' life do the

[1] Mk. 1:14.   [2] See below, pp. 18off.

Gospels again present a clear chronological scheme, and we shall follow their example.

It will be useful, however, to make here a few very general points about the over-all pattern of Jesus' activity, to provide a rough framework for the material in the next five chapters.

Time

John the Baptist started preaching probably in AD 28.[1] How long it was before Jesus came to be baptized, and how long after that Jesus and John continued their parallel ministry before John's imprisonment, we cannot be sure, but if we say it was about AD 30 or a little before when Jesus started preaching in Galilee, we shall not be far out. And from that point it was probably something over two years until his death.[2] So the events of the following chapters, with the rise and fall in Jesus' popularity and the growth of official opposition to him, should be seen as fitting into two or three years. No chronological detail is undisputed, but a ministry of roughly that length is commonly agreed.[3]

Place

We have already noticed that, while the first three Gospels speak only of Jesus' ministry in Galilee before his final visit to Jerusalem, John records much early activity in Judaea, probably preceding the preaching and healing mission in

[1] See above, p. 26, note 1.
[2] This is the usual inference from the fact that Mark seems to refer to two 'springtimes', in 2:23 (ripe corn) and 6:39 (green grass), besides the Passover festival when Jesus died (Passover was in the spring), and that John refers to three Passover festivals in 2:13; 6:4 and 12:1 (though the relevance of the first of these depends on the dating of the temple incident, which the other Gospels place at the Passover festival when Jesus died, *i.e.* the same Passover as John refers to in 12:1: see below, p. 131, note 1).
[3] If the Passover fell on a Friday in the year of Jesus' death (see below, p. 136, note 4), this would fit the astronomical data for AD 33, but not for AD 31 or 32. This further supports a ministry of about three years.

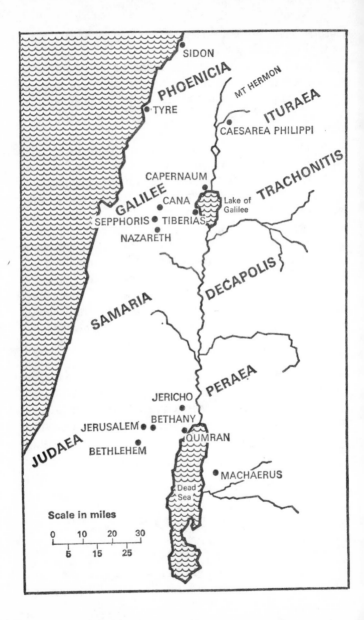

SIDON

PHOENICIA

MT HERMON

ITURAEA

TYRE

CAESAREA PHILIPPI

CAPERNAUM

GALILEE

TRACHONITIS

CANA

Lake of
Galilee

SEPPHORIS • TIBERIAS

NAZARETH

DECAPOLIS

SAMARIA

PERAEA

JERICHO

BETHANY

JERUSALEM

QUMRAN

JUDAEA

BETHLEHEM

MACHAERUS

Dead
Sea

Scale in miles

0   10   20   30

5   15   25

Galilee.[1] Even after Jesus' Galilean ministry begins, John records frequent visits to Jerusalem, so much so that in his Gospel there is considerably more activity set in Judaea than in Galilee even before the final week. Several of these visits to Jerusalem are said to be in connection with festivals,[2] and the discussion of Jesus with his brothers recorded in John 7:1–14 suggests that it was the regular practice for his family, as for many of the more orthodox Jews of Galilee, to make the pilgrimage to Jerusalem for the festivals.[3] The Judaean visits recorded by John therefore fit naturally as interludes in a period when his regular activity was in Galilee.

Apart from these occasional visits to Jerusalem, with the journeys through Samaria or the Jordan valley which they entailed, Jesus apparently stayed in Galilee for almost the whole period of his public activity after John's imprisonment. Three short journeys outside Galilee, one to the north into Phoenician territory and back via the Decapolis on the east side of the Lake of Galilee,[4] another to the north near Caesarea Philippi on the lower slopes of Mount Hermon,[5] and one across the Jordan to the scene of John's earlier activity,[6] probably represent deliberate periods of withdrawal from the constant exposure to public demand and debate which was inevitable in Galilee, or from the mounting threat of official reprisals. But Jesus was no global traveller: the whole of his ministry took place within an area of not more than 125 miles by 50, roughly the size of Devon and Cornwall, and most of it in only a small part of that area.

[1] See above, pp. 42, 43.
[2] Jn. 5:1; 7:1–14; 10:22.
[3] Cf. also Lk. 2:41, referring to the Passover; the festival in John 7 is Tabernacles.
[4] Mk. 7:24, 31.   [5] Mk. 8:27.
[6] Jn. 10:40.

Development

Without aiming at a detailed chronology, most scholars recognize that there were certain turning-points in Jesus' career.

We have already noticed how the arrest of John the Baptist was the signal for a change both in Jesus' area of operation and in his style of activity. The resultant Galilean ministry seems to have been a time of growing popularity, until this came to a climax, as we shall see in chapter 8, in the attempt of the Galilean crowd to make him king. Jesus reacted by withdrawing from the public eye, presumably to avoid a repetition of this very embarrassing popular misunderstanding of his mission, and concentrated instead on instructing his closest circle of followers. John the Baptist's execution at the same period may have been a further reason for avoiding too much publicity in a politically loaded situation.

This period of comparative seclusion led up to the 'retreat' to Caesarea Philippi, where his closest associates came to a more realistic awareness of the nature of his mission, and he began to prepare them for the inevitability of conflict, which would result in his death.[1] And so, amid growing popular bewilderment, perhaps disillusionment, at the strange attitude of their 'Messiah', and a growing awareness among his closest followers that his goal was not a crown but a cross, Jesus 'made up his mind and set out on his way to Jerusalem'[2] for the final confrontation. The story from that point on will be taken up in chapter 9.

This rough outline is all that the Gospels allow us to construct with confidence of the shape of Jesus' ministry from a strictly chronological point of view. But within that

[1] See below, pp. 116, 117.
[2] Lk. 9:51.

outline can be fitted an almost embarrassing wealth of detail which illustrates ever more clearly what that ministry was about, and it is with that wealth of detail that we shall be concerned in chapters 4–8.

4 Disciples

'Follow me,' said Jesus to four fishermen by the Lake of Galilee, and 'at once they left their nets and followed him'.[1] They knew what he meant. Every Jewish teacher worth his salt had his circle of 'disciples' who 'followed' him (literally walking behind him as he rode or walked ahead), looked after his daily needs, and soaked up his teaching. Their teacher was the most important person in their lives. 'Provide yourself with a teacher, and get yourself a companion,'[2] was an early Rabbi's advice to intending students of the Law, and the fellowship into which this association led was a close relationship of mutual care and respect. Another Rabbi summed it up: 'Let the honour of your disciple be as dear to you as your own, and as the honour of your companion, and the honour of your companion as the fear of your teacher, and the fear of your teacher as the fear of Heaven.'[3] It was into a relationship like that that Jesus was calling these four fishermen.

But that was just the difference: *he* was calling *them*. Jewish Rabbis did not call disciples to follow them: the

[1] Mk. 1:17, 18. The use of 'come with', 'went with' in TEV (verses 17, 18, 20) is misleading: in each case the Greek verb means explicitly 'follow' or 'go behind'.
[2] Mishnah, *Aboth* 1:6.   [3] Mishnah, *Aboth* 4:12.

disciples chose their own teachers and attached themselves to them. Yet all Jesus' disciples, that is his constant followers as opposed to the crowds who came to hear his teaching, seem to have been chosen by him. Indeed, he stressed this himself: 'You did not choose me; I chose you.'[1] We hear of three only who volunteered to follow Jesus, and all of them, if not flatly refused, got a very frosty reception.[2]

Nor was that the only difference. He was not calling them to a life of study, with the prospect of one day becoming teachers themselves. Not one of his disciples would have dreamt of trying to be another Jesus! He was calling them to join him in a mission which they did not fully understand, a mission which at first may have seemed glamorous, but was always dangerous, and was eventually to lead them into serious trouble. There was an element of learning, as we shall see, but following Jesus was essentially an existential commitment of their lives to certain goals and ideals, and above all to a person. It was Jesus, not his teaching, that was the object of their commitment. It was on Jesus himself, who he was and what he had done, that their teaching centred after he was gone.

The recruitment of the disciples

So Jesus began his Galilean ministry by gathering his first disciples. The readiness with which they left their family businesses is staggering. Could the impact of Jesus' personality have been so great that a mere word at their very first meeting was enough to change the course of their lives? Without wanting to belittle the impression Jesus clearly made on all sorts of people, we must notice that Mark has not told us the whole story. It was not the first time they had met. Back in the days when John was still

[1] Jn. 15:16.   [2] Lk. 9:57, 58, 61, 62; Mk. 5:18, 19.

baptizing, at least two of these fishermen, Simon and Andrew, perhaps all four,[1] had been drawn into the movement and had met Jesus.[2] Andrew at least was already convinced of Jesus' unique importance, and it seems that the little group had followed the news of Jesus' activities, and was well prepared to drop everything when the time came.

The four fishermen were only the beginning of a steady succession of recruits to Jesus' entourage. In a few cases the Gospels tell us how they joined the group, but in most cases we can only assume that, like the four fishermen and like Matthew the tax-collector,[3] they were confronted by the uncompromising demand, 'Follow me', and could not refuse.

They were a strange assortment. Only a few are known to us in any detail, but those few present some fascinating contrasts. James and John, nicknamed 'Sons of Thunder', were dominant and ambitious; Andrew, the first convert, was soon overshadowed by his more extrovert brother and seems to have been a steady 'back-room boy'. Philip, the eager follower who needs no second call, contrasts with his more sceptical friend Nathanael, and still more with the dogged pessimism of Thomas. Most unexpected of all, we find in the same group Simon the Zealot, who, if his nickname is to be taken literally, was implacably opposed to compromise with Rome,[4] and Matthew who, as a tax-collector, could expect to be cordially detested as a collaborator. Jesus was then, as now, capable of appealing to people of widely different temperaments and backgrounds,

[1] Many believe that the unnamed companion of Andrew in Jn. 1:35–40 was John, son of Zebedee, who with his brother James was a business partner of Simon and Andrew (Lk. 5:10).
[2] Jn. 1:35–42.   [3] Mt. 9:9.
[4] See below, p. 108, note 2. Even if *zēlōtēs* refers primarily to zeal for the Law of God, his views would be sharply opposed to those of an imperial tax-collector.

and of instilling into them a common loyalty which made lesser divisions irrelevant.

Most of the inner circle seem to have been from the same 'middle-class' background as Jesus. The four fishermen were partners in a business thriving enough to employ workers,[1] and Thomas and Nathanael were in the same line of business.[2] Luke records that among Jesus' entourage were some women sufficiently wealthy to contribute to the group's support from their own pockets.[3] Matthew the tax-collector would have needed a reasonable degree of education to qualify for his influential job, and all that we know of the later teaching of the apostles suggests men with a sound education in Old Testament Scripture, though, like Jesus, without the paper qualifications of a Rabbinic schooling.[4]

All of the inner circle except one seem to have been Galileans. Most of their names are Jewish, but Andrew and Philip are Greek names, and it is interesting that it was these two who were responsible for a significant meeting of Jesus with Greek enquirers.[5] This is not to suggest that Andrew and Philip were themselves Gentiles; certainly not. But their inclusion, like that of Matthew, may indicate that Jesus' following was drawn not only from the more strictly orthodox element in Galilean Judaism, but also from the more liberal 'Hellenistic' element.

The one non-Galilean, probably, was Judas Iscariot. His name has usually been interpreted, following several early Greek manuscripts, as meaning 'man of Kerioth'. If so, he was from either Kerioth in Moab, on the east of the Dead Sea, or, more likely, Kerioth-Hezron in the deep

[1] Mk. 1:20.   [2] Jn. 21:2, 3.   [3] Lk. 8:3.
[4] 'Ordinary men of no education' (Acts 4:13) does not mean that they were illiterate, but that as laymen they lacked the formal scribal education normally expected in a Sanhedrin debate.
[5] Jn. 12:20–22.

south of Judaea. In view of his eventual treachery, it is no wonder that the Gospels always portray him as the odd man out; but it may well be that he never really felt at home among this motley crowd of Galileans. Many motives for his *volte-face* have been suggested, but it is possible that a Judaean disdain for an essentially Galilean movement was among them.

The Twelve

We have spoken several times of the 'inner circle' of Jesus' disciples. Four concentric circles need to be distinguished: the crowds who came and went, moved by the teaching and miracles of Jesus, but essentially spectators; the 'disciples' as a whole, those who, probably with varying degrees of seriousness, committed themselves to follow Jesus; the 'inner circle' of the Twelve, selected by Jesus from among the disciples; and the most intimate group of three, Peter, James and John, who were permitted by Jesus to share in some of the highest moments of his ministry,[1] and who were recognized as leading members even of the inner circle of the Twelve.

Jesus' selection of the Twelve was one of his key decisions. The fact that he spent a whole night in prayer before making the choice indicates how important it was for him.[2] These were the men on whose training much of his attention would be focused, and on whom the continuation of his mission would depend. It was with this inner circle that Jesus shared his last meal, as they had shared so many meals and so many experiences before. It was they who became the first leaders of the Christian movement.

Mark sums up the function of the Twelve in three

[1] Mk. 5:37; 9:2; 14:33; *cf.* also 13:3.
[2] Lk. 6:12, 13.

phrases: to be with him; to be sent out preaching; and to have authority to exorcize demons.[1]

The mission of the Twelve

The last two of these functions were soon put to use: Jesus sent out the Twelve on a preaching and healing mission.[2] Very likely there were several such campaigns by the Twelve; only one is specifically recorded, but Luke mentions a subsequent mission involving seventy-two disciples, and this probably indicates that the recorded mission of the Twelve was not a once-for-all experiment. Jesus had called his first four disciples from catching fish to 'catch men',[3] and it was particularly through such missions that they could do so.

Their mission was in effect an extension of Jesus' ministry. His preaching focused on the good news that the Kingdom of God had come; it was the proclamation of a quite new state of affairs between man and God, and required a decisive response of repentance and acceptance. Just what the 'Kingdom of God' meant we shall consider later;[4] but clearly there was an urgency about Jesus' preaching. Now the disciples were sent out with the same message,[5] and with a sense of urgency so great that they were forbidden even to observe the normal courtesies which are so important to travellers in the East.[6] They were to travel light, and depend on finding hospitality with sympathizers.[7] Where they met with no response, they were not to waste time on argument, still less on pleasantries, but to move on.[8]

And as they went they not only preached but healed and

[1] Mk. 3:14, 15. [2] Mt. 10:5–15. [3] Mk. 1:17.
[4] See below, chapter 8, especially pp. 123–125.
[5] Mt. 10:7; Mk. 6:12; cf. the summary of Jesus' preaching in Mk. 1:14, 15. [6] Lk. 10:4. [7] Mt. 10:9–11.
[8] Mt. 10:14.

exorcized demons, just as Jesus did.[1] We shall see in the next chapter how significant such healing was: it was a sign of the arrival of the Kingdom of God. The matter-of-fact way in which the Gospels mention exorcism and miraculous healing by the disciples is staggering:[2] it looks as if it was an expected part of such a mission. Certainly it must have added considerable weight to their preaching. The large popular following which Jesus had, at least during the earlier part of his ministry in Galilee, was probably due in large measure to the effectiveness of his disciples' campaign.

The heart of discipleship

But all this hectic activity accounts for only the second and third of Mark's three phrases. Before preaching and exorcism, and necessarily prior to them, comes the first element in discipleship, 'to be with him'. They were not propagandists of a political creed, but adherents, and ambassadors, of a *person*, and their relationship with him was the secret of their effectiveness. We have noted how Jesus devoted more and more time to teaching and preparing them as his ministry went on. Mark tells us how, after the mission of the Twelve, Jesus deliberately withdrew with them into a lonely place to escape the crowds.[3] They needed a rest, after the physical and emotional demands of their tour; but just as important was the need for them to take stock of their position, and for Jesus to continue the teaching without which such missions would be useless.

This particular attempt to escape was a failure, but it was followed by others,[4] and it seems that such 'retreats' were a regular feature of their life together. Only so could Jesus have given all the private teaching to his disciples which

[1] Mk. 6:13. [2] Mt. 10:8 even includes raising the dead.
[3] Mk. 6:30–32.
[4] See above, p. 47; *cf.* Mk. 9:30, 31: 'Jesus did not want anyone to know where he was, *because* he was teaching his disciples . . .'

the Gospels record. John's long account of the instruction and encouragement given by Jesus to the Twelve (or rather Eleven!) at the Last Supper[1] is typical of the sort of training sessions they must often have had before.

They proved slow learners, the Gospels tell us.[2] Even by the time of Jesus' death they did not really understand what was going on, and the resurrection took them completely by surprise. Then at last the truth began to dawn on them, and Jesus' patient teaching, remembered but not yet understood, began to come to life as well. They had learnt their lessons well, and before long the loyal activists in a dimly understood cause became the theological brains behind the world's most successful ideological movement. But all because they had first 'been with him'; at the heart of their ideology was the Jesus they had lived with, and the paramount importance of a vital relationship with him as the secret of the Kingdom of God.

All or nothing

What did it really mean to be a disciple of Jesus ? His teaching to his disciples gives us the ingredients for quite a full – and sobering – answer.

It was all or nothing. 'No one can be a slave to two masters: ... You cannot serve both God and money.'[3] And it was not only money that might prove a counter-attraction. Even the most natural and binding of human loyalty must give way: 'Whoever loves his father or mother more than me is not worthy of me; whoever loves his son or daughter more than me is not worthy of me.'[4] An eager would-be disciple was deliberately and quite abruptly put off when he asked permission to go and say goodbye to his family: 'Anyone who starts to plough and then keeps

[1] Jn. 13–16. [2] See, *e.g.*, Mk. 8:17–21; 9:10, 32; Jn. 12:16.
[3] Mt. 6:24. [4] Mt. 10:37.

looking back is of no use for the Kingdom of God.'[1]

To accept the call to discipleship was, in a sense, to give up your life.[2] It was like joining a funeral procession – your own! The sight of a criminal on his way to execution, forced to carry his own gibbet and exposed to the mockery of onlookers, was familiar enough in Roman Palestine. Jesus saw it as an illustration of discipleship: 'If anyone wants to come after me, he must forget himself, carry his cross, and follow me.'[3] A potent enough illustration, even before Jesus himself gave it flesh and blood. Discipleship was not for the squeamish, or for those who cared too much what others thought of them.

Odd man out

Jesus always insisted that anyone who followed him was bound to be conspicuous, simply because he would be as different from other men as light from darkness. Indeed, on this very distinctiveness his usefulness depended. 'You are like salt for all mankind. But if salt loses its taste, there is no way to make it salty again. It has become worthless; ... You are like the light for the world. ... Nobody lights a lamp to put it under a bowl; instead he puts it on the lamp-stand, where it gives light for everyone in the house. In the same way your light must shine before people, so that they will see the good things you do and give praise to your Father in heaven.'[4]

It is significant that these words come immediately after the much-loved but much-misunderstood 'Beatitudes' of Matthew 5:3–12. In this portrait of the 'happy' man, Jesus is not giving a universal recipe for contentment, but a description of life in the Kingdom of God, the life of a Christian disciple. And it is about as far removed from the ethos of secular society as possible. Spiritual humility, a

[1] Lk. 9:62. [2] Mk. 8:35. [3] Mk. 8:34. [4] Mt. 5:13–16.

sensitive seriousness, meekness (giving way to the other man), a consuming desire for what is right, mercy, purity, conciliation, and a joyful willingness to accept insult and injury as the price of loyalty to God, these are not the dominant characteristics of human society as we know it! They are not even the ideals which secular man would claim to aspire to. Men like this will be conspicuous, and Jesus made no bones about it. That is what disciples are for, to be noticed.

But no-one loves the odd man out, especially when he feels the comparison is not in his own favour. So here in the Beatitudes and in many other places in Jesus' teaching there is the warning that discipleship will mean unpopularity, and worse.[1] Jesus was to be hated, hounded, and eventually tortured to death, and his followers need not hope for any better treatment. 'Everyone will hate you, because of me,' he said.

But even under persecution the distinctive character of a disciple of Jesus was to come to the fore. They should be glad to be treated as true men of God had always been: 'Happy are you when men hate you, and reject you, and insult you, and say that you are evil, because of the Son of Man! Be happy when that happens, and dance for joy, for a great reward is kept for you in heaven. For their ancestors did the very same things to the prophets.'[2] They should not retaliate. Indeed they should love those who ill-treated them, and pray for them. There was to be no limit to their forgiveness, for friend or enemy.[3] One of the most exasperating characteristics of Christians has always been that they don't easily respond in kind to hatred and ill-treatment: love and forgiveness can be quite un-nerving! But that was how Jesus meant it to be.

[1] E.g. Mt. 10:16–25; Jn. 15:18–21.   [2] Lk. 6:22, 23.
[3] Mt. 5:38–48; 18:21, 22.

Love one another

If they were to love and forgive their 'enemies', it is hardly surprising that Jesus also stressed the need to love each other within the group of disciples. He called this his 'new commandment'; if they kept it, everyone would know that they were his disciples.[1]

But love is not just a warm fellow-feeling. Jesus laid down this 'new commandment' just after he had given a striking demonstration of what he meant by love. He had just gone round the circle of the disciples, washing their feet! He, the Master, doing the slave's job! There was no room for self-importance in Jesus' circle. Humble, unselfish service was the mark of greatness. Jockeying for position was unthinkable.

Jesus had no time for the rat-race. Several times we read in the Gospels of disputes among the disciples about which of them was the greatest, and there were few failings which provoked such sharp rebukes from Jesus as this. 'You know that the men who are considered rulers of the people lord it over them, and the leaders exercise authority over them. This, however, is not the way it is among you. If one of you wants to be great, he must be the servant of the rest; and if one of you wants to be first, he must be the slave of all.'[2] More than once he commended the example of children: 'Unless you change and become like children, you will never enter the Kingdom of heaven. The greatest in the Kingdom of heaven is the one who humbles himself and becomes like this child.'[3] Following Jesus is not meant to be a flattering occupation!

God first

Jesus had some hard words to say about people who are chiefly concerned about the sort of impression they make

[1] Jn. 13:34, 35.   [2] Mk. 10:42-44.   [3] Mt. 18:3, 4.

60

on others, especially in matters of religion, men who choose the most conspicuous places to pray and must have a fanfare before they give a donation. His disciples must avoid ostentation, caring only for what *God* thought of them.[1] For the key to the remarkable attitude to both friends and enemies that Jesus demanded was their attitude to God.

God must take the first place in a disciple's loyalty. They were to regard him as their Father, always anxious to please him, and trusting him absolutely for all they needed. Did not God provide for the birds and the flowers? Then he would provide for them. Worry was forbidden; faith must take its place. For the man of faith there was no limit to the good things he could expect his Father to give him, provided only that he put God first.[2]

It was this God-ward orientation which lay behind the distinctive character which Jesus demanded of his disciples. The Beatitudes describe a man who puts God first. This is the key to unselfishness, and unselfishness is another word for love. It is only in this way that a man can really love his enemies, and happily accept a humble position as the reward for seniority.

The demands of discipleship

All this is so contrary to our natural self-centredness that it is not surprising that the demands Jesus made on his disciples proved too much for them. Some never even started, like the rich man to whom Jesus made it clear that his money must take second place.[3] Others joined the band-wagon in the early days, but jumped off again as Jesus' real intentions became clear.[4] In the end, when the

[1] Mt. 6:1–18.
[2] See especially Mt. 6:24–34; 7:7–11.
[3] Mk. 10:17–22.
[4] Jn. 6:66. See below, p. 110, for the significance of this desertion.

crunch came, even Peter, the loyal lieutenant, denied ever having met Jesus, and the rest of them ran away before they had to face the challenge.

Jesus expected this. He warned them in two crisp parables that it would not be easy to be a disciple. He pictures the builder who starts a job without working out if he can afford to finish it, and the king who goes to war and finds himself facing an army twice the size of his own. 'In the same way none of you can be my disciple unless he gives up everything he has.'[1] Better not to start than to face the humiliation of failure.

All this seems a far cry from present-day Christian discipleship as we know it in the West, where ministers' energy is devoted to inducing people to join up, not to dissuading them, where discipleship seems to cost nothing but an occasional modest financial contribution, if even that, and where the only obvious difference between the average Christian and his neighbours is his strange habit of going out to church on Sunday mornings. Of course the present-day disciple cannot be called literally to give up his home to travel round with Jesus, and he will probably not be sent out to exorcize demons. But we may well wonder what has happened to the all-or-nothing commitment Jesus demanded, the conspicuously different way of life outlined in the Beatitudes, the mutual love and humility, and the practical day-to-day dependence on God which were to be the hallmark of those who followed Jesus. 'A city built on a high hill cannot be hidden', said Jesus,[2] but modern Western Christianity seems to have perfected the art of camouflage.

The privilege of the disciple
But it is not only on the demands of discipleship that we

[1] Lk. 14:28–33.   [2] Mt. 5:14.

are missing out. What we have said so far might suggest that following Jesus was meant to be a grim, unrewarding business, a reluctant acceptance of the call of duty. That is what some Christians have tried to make it. But not Jesus. In contrast with the dour righteousness of the Pharisees, there is an overwhelming note of joy in Jesus' idea of discipleship. Indeed this was one of the things they objected to: why couldn't Jesus' disciples fast like all respectable religious people? Jesus' reply is characteristic. Can you expect the guests at a wedding to fast?! He went on to describe his way of life as like new wine, powerful and effervescent, which would only explode the old wineskins of traditional formal religion if they tried to contain it. Jesus, and his 'religion', was irrepressible.[1]

The wedding-feast image comes up several times in Jesus' descriptions of what it means to be his disciple.[2] Or he pictures it as like discovering a priceless treasure.[3] It is joy that is the dominant note in his parables of the lost sheep, the lost coin and the lost son.[4] Jesus himself had a reputation for conviviality in contrast to John the Baptist.[5] He expected his disciples to be happy, even in the face of persecution.[6]

What was there to be so happy about? There was, first, the sheer privilege of being recognized as a representative of Jesus, because, as they came increasingly to realize, that made them no less than representatives of God.[7] Indeed, Jesus went so far as to refer to his faithful followers as his own family, closer to him than his mother and his brothers.[8]

But some of them had given up a lot to follow Jesus; was there to be no compensation? Peter, never a prey to false

---

[1] Mk. 2:18–22.
[2] *E.g.* Mt. 22:2–14; 25:1–12; *cf.* the banquet idea in Mt. 8:11; Lk. 22:30.   [3] Mt. 13:44–46.   [4] Lk. 15:5–7, 9,10, 22–24.
[5] Mt. 11: 16–19.   [6] Mt. 5:10–12.
[7] Mt. 10:40–42; Lk. 10:16.   [8] Mk. 3:34, 35; *cf.* Lk. 11:27, 28.

modesty, put it to Jesus squarely: ' "Look, we have left everything and followed you." "Yes," Jesus said to them, "and I tell you this: anyone who leaves home or brothers or sisters or mother or father or children or fields for me, and for the gospel, will receive much more in this present age. He will receive a hundred times more houses, brothers, sisters, mothers, children, and fields – and persecutions as well; and in the age to come he will receive eternal life." ' [1] A hundredfold compensation in this life? Did Jesus really mean that? Most of them never seem to have regained the security of the family business, let alone a 10,000% profit!

But they did gain something else. The disciples were a close-knit group, characterized by mutual love and concern, which soon expressed itself practically in a sharing of money and goods, often described as 'Christian communism'. In this close relationship, with its common sense of purpose, they found not only material security, but a new and greater family. Ever since then, one of the things which has most attracted people to the Christian faith has been the warmth of the fellowship they have seen among those who take their discipleship seriously, and no true Christian has found that any loss which his discipleship entailed proved to be a bad bargain. Compensation 'in this present age'? Yes, a hundred times over!

'And in the age to come he will receive eternal life.' Pie in the sky when you die? Yes, though most disciples would claim that they have had a fair slice of the pie even before that! But Jesus' message, as we shall see in chapter 8, *was* focused on an other-worldly fulfilment, and in that other world the disciple would find his place. 'You have stayed with me all through my trials;' said Jesus to the Twelve, 'and just as my Father has given me the right to

[1] Mk. 10:28–30.

rule, so I will make the same agreement with you. You will eat and drink at my table in my Kingdom, and you will sit on thrones to judge the twelve tribes of Israel.'[1] 'Compensation' is too weak a word!

But in any case talk of compensation misses the point. Following Jesus, for all the demands it entails, is not a sacrifice; it is a privilege. It is the passport to a relationship with God which amounts to nothing less than a new life. John has recorded for us Jesus' summary of what he came to do: 'I have come in order that they might have life, life in all its fulness.'[2] Life after death, yes; but also life here and now which makes ordinary existence look pale.

Big claims, and big demands! It is a measure of the greatness of Jesus that he could make such claims and such demands, and expect to be taken seriously. That he was taken seriously, not only by some of his contemporaries, but by increasing numbers ever since who have 'left their nets and followed him', suggests that Jesus is a force to be reckoned with.

[1] Lk. 22:28–30.   [2] Jn. 10:10.

5 Miracles

'Miracles', said Matthew Arnold, 'do not happen'; and I suppose most modern men and women would agree with him. So they find the Gospels heavy going, because the Gospels are full of miracles.

There was a time when scholars took the easy way out, and simply cut out all the miracles. They were impossible, so they could not have happened. What was left was a Jesus who, if unremarkable, was at least inoffensive to the secular mind.

But more recent scholarship has realized that this will not do. The miracles are not just a supernatural varnish added by pious believers to the story of a pedestrian preaching ministry. They are deeply embedded in all the strata of tradition which scholars have detected behind the writing of the Gospels. Moreover, much of Jesus' teaching presupposes his miracles, and would make nonsense without them. Preaching and miracles cannot be separated; together they make up a coherent account of the ministry of Jesus as a total onslaught on the powers of evil. Whatever varying traits modern scholars may emphasize in their portraits of Jesus, one feature on which practically all are now agreed is that Jesus became famous partly, if not chiefly, as a worker of miracles. Even the subsequent Jewish polemic against Jesus backs this up, in that he is presented as a sorcerer – not the most likely stick with which to beat a mere preacher of ethics! So I make no apology for devoting a chapter to this aspect of the life and work of Jesus.

Later in the chapter we shall have to consider the significance of the miracles, not least to the steadily increasing ranks of the Matthew Arnolds. But before we can talk meaningfully about their significance, we need to get clear what sort of miracles we are talking about.

Healing miracles

By far the commonest type of miracle in the Gospel stories is miraculous healing. It was as a healer and exorcist that Jesus was famous. There are about twenty healings and six exorcisms individually recorded in the Gospels, besides several general statements about the large numbers healed by Jesus.[1] Clearly we cannot hope to look at all these in detail.

Jesus cured a wide variety of complaints. Making due allowance for the imprecise medical terminology of the Gospels, we may distinguish various forms of paralysis, congenital defects like blindness, deafness and dumbness, diseases like leprosy, dropsy and fever, haemorrhage, curvature of the spine, and a severed ear. If even half of these are correctly diagnosed, the Gospel account of Jesus healing 'all kinds of diseases' seems no exaggeration. There are even three accounts of Jesus restoring to life someone who had recently died.[2]

His methods varied almost as widely as the complaints he dealt with. Usually, though not always, there was a word

[1] *E.g.* Mk. 1:32–34; 3:7–12; 6:55, 56; Lk. 7:21, 22.
[2] Mk. 5:35–43; Lk. 7:11–16; Jn. 11:1–44.

of command, 'Be healed', or the like. Sometimes, as far as the accounts go, that was all: no ritual, no manipulation, just a word of authority. In fact so famous was Jesus for this word of command that an army officer once phrased his request for healing like this: 'Just give the order and my servant will get well. I, too, am a man with superior officers over me, and I have soldiers under me; so I order this one, "Go!" and he goes; and I order that one, "Come!" and he comes; and I order my slave, "Do this!" and he does it.'[1] Jesus had a reputation for having the same authority over disease that an officer has over his subordinates! In fact we are told that on this occasion, and two others, Jesus did 'just give the order' without even going to the patient, and the cure was immediately effective.[2]

But usually he stood by a person when he healed him, and often we are told that he touched them, laid his hands on them, or took them by the hand. Occasionally he used a more elaborate technique, involving the use of spittle,[3] which, strange as it seems to us, was quite commonly used by both Jewish and pagan healers. But these were exceptions; generally there was a minimum of fuss and ritual.

One interesting case concerns a woman whose haemorrhage was cured when she merely touched Jesus' cloak. He did not see her coming, but was immediately aware that something had happened: 'power had gone out of him.'[4] Apparently others too were cured by merely touching Jesus or his clothes.[5] The impression is of an irrepressible healing power which could operate even without Jesus' express desire.

All this might sound rather mechanical, even magical, but for the one factor in the equation which we have not

[1] Mt. 8:8, 9.　　　　[2] See also Mk. 7:24–30; Jn. 4:46–53.
[3] Mk. 7:33; 8:23; Jn. 9:6, 7.　　　　[4] Mk. 5:25–34.
[5] Mk. 6:56; Lk. 6:19.

68

yet mentioned – faith. Jesus told the woman who had been cured by touching his cloak, 'Your faith has made you well.' Many of the healing stories emphasize the faith either of the patient or of those who asked for the cure on his behalf. Where there is faith, there is no limit to what can be done;[1] where there is no faith, there is no healing.[2] The key to Jesus' healing power was not a magical ritual, but a relationship of trust, based on a firm conviction of his power over illness. When the army officer made his famous statement about the authority of Jesus, it was for his 'faith' that Jesus commended him, and in response to his 'faith' that he healed his servant.[3] Details of method are scarcely relevant. The over-all impression is of the overwhelming authority of Jesus, deployed in response to faith to meet genuine human need as it confronted him, in whatever way was most appropriate to the case.

There is nothing of the exhibitionism about Jesus which seems to have characterized most of the magical or 'spiritual' healers of his day, and indeed many in our own day. He did not set out on 'healing campaigns', but simply dealt with real needs when he met them. He did not go looking for potential 'subjects': in most cases it was the patients or their relatives who took the initiative and came to him. On some occasions he deliberately avoided spectators.[4] This was not a travelling circus, but a man of extraordinary power engaged in a battle against evil not only on the spiritual but also on the physical plane.

Exorcisms

That last sentence might suggest that the physical and the spiritual are quite separate areas of reality. In fact, however, modern medicine is increasingly realizing the danger

[1] Mk. 9:23. [2] Mk. 6:5, 6. [3] Mt. 8:10, 13.
[4] E.g. Mk. 5:37; 7:33; 8:23.

of making such a rigid distinction, and words like 'psycho-somatic' are in vogue. In New Testament days there was certainly no such distinction. Hence the need to go on now to another aspect of Jesus' healing ministry, exorcism.

If most people still find it difficult to take miraculous healing seriously, exorcism is inevitably even more suspect. At least we all know that physical illness is a reality, whatever reservations we may have about miraculous cures; but demons and evil spirits are not part of everyday experience for most of us, at least in the Western world.

In many parts of the world it is not so. In West Africa, where I have recently been living, it is not only among the uneducated that the dimension of spiritual powers is recognized. Even among university students and lecturers a real fear of witchcraft and evil spirits lies only just below the surface. Sometimes it comes into the open, and not only in psychological disturbances, but in very tangible manifestations of spiritual forces which secular man would prefer to ignore.

And now even in the 'civilized' West it is hard to confine the demonic to the cosy make-believe of ghost-stories. Interest in occult practices is increasing steadily, and correspondingly exorcism is coming back into its own, not only in sensational films but in sober experience. Those who have met Satanism in British universities are not likely to sneer again at the possibility of demon-possession.

At any rate, in first-century Palestine it was a serious concern. The professional exorcist was a recognized figure, and several famous Rabbis are credited with feats of exorcism as well as miraculous healings.[1] It was to be expected that Jesus, as a campaigner against evil, should

[1] For exorcists outside the Christian group see Mk. 9:38; Acts 19:13–16. There are numerous references to Jewish exorcists in Josephus and in Rabbinic literature: see G. Vermes, *Jesus the Jew* (Collins, 1973), pp. 63–68.

practise exorcism. In addition to the half-dozen specific cases narrated, several general summaries of Jesus' healing ministry in the Gospels include exorcism as a regular part of that ministry.[1] It was his fame as an exorcist which led to one of his brushes with the Jerusalem establishment.[2] Even his disciples were expected to be exorcists,[3] though their rate of success was not equal to his.[4]

The distinction between 'ordinary' diseases and demonic attacks is not always clearly drawn in the Gospels. One case of demon-possession looks very much like what we would call epilepsy,[5] and occasionally blindness and dumbness are attributed to a demon.[6] But usually a clear distinction is drawn between exorcism and the healing of 'medical' complaints;[7] nearly all the accounts of ordinary healings make no mention of demons,[8] while in most accounts of exorcism no identifiable complaint is mentioned, just 'possession' by a demon, with resultant abnormalities in behaviour, not physical defects. The cure consists of the demon 'coming out', after which the patient returns to normality.

The distinction is seen also in Jesus' method of healing. In exorcism Jesus did not, as far as our records go, touch the patient, as he frequently did in ordinary healings. The exorcism is done by a word of command alone.[9] It is a conflict of wills between Jesus and the demon, with the 'patient' involved only as the battleground of the two spiritual forces. Where faith is mentioned, it is the faith of the victim's father or mother, not of the victim himself,

[1] *E.g.* Mk. 1:34, 39; 3:11, 12; Lk. 7:21.
[2] Mk. 3:22–30.　　　[3] Mk. 3:15; 6:7, 13; Lk. 10:17.
[4] Mk. 9:14–29.　　　[5] Mk. 9:17–27.　　　[6] Mt. 9:32, 33; 12:22.
[7] *E.g.* Mk. 1:32, 34; 3:10, 11; Lk. 13:32; *cf.* Acts 8:7.
[8] To attribute a disease to Satanic origin, as in Lk. 13:16, is not the same as to attribute it to a 'resident' demon.
[9] Note how Mt. 8:16 makes this distinction: 'Jesus drove out the evil spirits with a word and healed all who were sick.'

who seems to play no conscious part in the operation.

As with the healings discussed above, there is a clear contrast between the naked simplicity of Jesus' challenge to the demons and the elaborate ritual indulged in by other Jewish exorcists, involving rings, herbs, smoke, and quasimagical incantations. Again the dominant note is of the incontestable authority of Jesus. 'What is this? Some kind of new teaching? This man has authority to give orders to the evil spirits, and they obey him!'[1]

Nature miracles

When we turn to Jesus' other miracles, besides healings and exorcisms, it may come as a surprise to find how few are recorded by comparison. It was as a healer and exorcist that Jesus was famous, not as a general worker of miracles. The Gospels, for all their emphasis on the healing ministry of Jesus, record only eight other miracles between them.

Five are concerned with a miraculous supply of food or drink to meet a real shortage (two large crowds fed, each from a single lunch-packet; two large catches of fish from a lake that had hitherto defied the best efforts of the experts;[2] and wine supplied at a wedding feast from pots of water); two demonstrate Jesus' control over the elements (a storm on the lake stopped by a word of command, and Jesus' ability to walk on the water); and one concerns a seemingly unnecessary curse placed on a fruitless fig-tree, which died as a result.[3]

[1] Mk. 1:27.
[2] Both in the cases of feeding a crowd (Mk. 6:35–44; 8:1–9) and in the miraculous catches of fish (Lk. 5:4–11; Jn. 21:1–11) it is often suggested that the two stories of each type are duplicate accounts of the same event. There are, however, significant differences in each case, sufficient to make a repetition of the same kind of miracle the more probable explanation.
[3] I have not listed the incident of the coin in the fish's mouth (Mt. 17:27), as there is in fact no miracle recorded there: Jesus' proposal to Peter is not said to have been carried out, and it has been suggested that

In most cases, then, these miracles were Jesus' way of meeting a real emergency; only the walking on the water and the curse of the fig-tree have no immediately useful purpose, but were apparently designed to impress upon the disciples the power available to those who have faith.[1] While these nature miracles did of course serve to convince the disciples of the unique authority of Jesus over inanimate nature as well as over rational beings, human and spiritual, they do not give the impression of being deliberately designed as displays of power. They arise, like the healings and exorcisms, out of real-life situations, and are the 'natural' response of Jesus to those situations. It is just that Jesus *was* different, not that he went out of his way to prove it.

Fact or fiction?

We have seen that modern scholars are agreed, with few exceptions, that Jesus was known in his day as a miracle-worker. This is not, however, to say that he actually worked miracles! The historical evidence for Jesus' miracles in general is in fact as strong as could be expected for any event in that historical context, though naturally the degree of direct testimony and circumstantial detail varies from one incident to another. But for some people no amount of historical evidence is sufficient to prove such an improbable event as a departure from the normal cause-and-effect pattern which has come to be dignified by the name

---

it was a playful comment, based on a popular story-motif found in both pagan and Jewish sources (Herodotus iii. 42; Babylonian Talmud, *Shabbath* 119a), and not meant to be taken very seriously. The whole episode is designed not to record a miracle, but to tell us Jesus' attitude towards the payment of religious taxes.
[1] Note that in both cases Jesus makes it clear that the power to work the miracle is available to his disciples as well: Mt. 14:28–31; Mk. 11:21–23. The fig-tree episode is also sometimes explained as an 'acted parable' of God's judgment on fruitless Israel.

of 'natural law'. Miracles do not happen, so there *must* be some other explanation.

And so we get all the ingenious 'explanations' which have long been familiar to students of the Gospels: Jesus did not feed five thousand people with one lunch-packet, but the unselfish action of one youngster shamed others in the crowd into sharing their lunches as well; he did not walk on the water, but only waded in the surf near the shore; Jairus' daughter was not dead, but in a coma, and so on. Such explanations are not new. 'They say miracles are past;' says Lafeu in *All's Well that Ends Well*, 'and we have our philosophical persons to make modern and familiar things supernatural and causeless.' That was nearly four centuries ago, and they are still at it!

Scientific knowledge can, of course, throw valuable light on the way the miracles may have happened. The Lake of Galilee, because of its surrounding high hills split by valleys which act as funnels for the wind, is known to be subject to sudden violent squalls which die away as quickly as they blow up. But if that was all that happened, why did they bother to tell the story at all? The point was that the storm dropped just when Jesus told it to. Coincidence? But it does not take many pages of the Gospels to stretch 'coincidnece' to the limits.

Similarly the increasing recognition in modern medicine that the mind affects the working of the body, as well as *vice versa*, makes it considerably easier to understand many of the healing miracles of Jesus. But no-one could pretend that they can be simply explained *away* as a precocious experiment in psychosomatic medicine. Few of the miracle stories in the Gospels could be paralleled from the case-book of a modern doctor, or even psychiatrist. Scientific explanations may help us to read between the lines, but they will never eliminate the very considerable deposit of miracle from the Gospels. Unless it is all sheer fiction, Jesus frequently did do things which fall outside the scope of natural science.

His contemporary opponents did not believe it was fiction, and so they put forward their own explanation: 'It is Beelzebul, the chief of the demons, who gives him the power to drive them out.'[1] It was absurd, of course, as Jesus was quick to point out, to suggest that Beelzebul would use Jesus to attack his own 'troops', but the charge was not dropped, and Jewish writers continued to portray Jesus as a sorcerer or magician using Satanic powers, and even came to regard this as one of the charges on which he was condemned to death.[2] This earliest 'explanation' of Jesus' miracles has at least the merit that it tries to provide a suitably supernatural source for a power which was recognized as miraculous, but it need hardly be said that no-one who has read the Gospels can imagine the Jesus they present as a mere magician, still less as a tool of Satan!

So in the end we come back to the same choice which faced us in connection with the miraculous birth of Jesus. Either you accept that 'natural law', for all its undoubted validity as a guide for living, cannot pretend to be a total account of the possibilities, in other words that miracles can and do happen; or you stick to your secular guns, and refuse, whatever the evidence, to admit an event which cannot at least in principle be explained by natural science: miracles do not happen, and anyone who says they did, or do, is a fool or a liar.

So it all depends on your view of the world, whether you cannot conceive of history, and life, as more than a 'closed continuum of effects', or you are open to a reality broader than most modern men find in their everyday experience. The story of Jesus will not boil down into secular terms.

[1] Lk. 11:15.   [2] Babylonian Talmud, *Sanhedrin* 43a.

The closed mind has no option but to reject much of the best-attested historical material as fiction. But in most areas of study it is evidence which is supposed to control hypotheses, not *vice versa*, and that is why there are many for whom the hypothesis of a purely secular universe has proved too tight, and who, however much they may debate the authenticity of this or that incident, find it impossible to explain Jesus without admitting that miracles can, and did, happen.[1]

The meaning of the miracles

If we may grant that Jesus did in fact work the sort of miracles the Gospels record, the more important question is what this indicates about Jesus and his mission.

We should notice first that Jesus' miracles were not normally done to *prove* anything, though there are exceptions.[2] When asked to give a 'sign' to order in support of his claims, he refused point blank.[3] Generally his miracles were the immediate response of Jesus to a real need as it confronted him. Sometimes, as we have seen, he went out of his way to avoid an audience, and several times he even told the patient not to talk about his cure.[4] But while they may not have been *designed* as demonstrations, the miracles were seen from the very beginning, even by Jesus himself, to have a very important significance; so much so that John's word for them is 'signs'.[5]

Of course the mere fact of miraculous healing was not in

[1] See further, below, pp. 169, 170, on the resurrection.
[2] Mk. 2:10–12; Lk. 7:20–23.   [3] Mk. 8:11–13; Mt. 16:1–4.
[4] *E.g.* Mk. 1:44; 5:43; 7:36.
[5] Most of the miracles recorded by John are made the occasion for teaching on the spiritual role of Jesus, for which the miracle serves as an acted parable ('sign'): thus the healing of a blind man leads to teaching on spiritual blindness (chapter 9), and the feeding of the five thousand to teaching on Jesus as the source of spiritual sustenance (chapter 6). But they are also 'signs' in the sense of revealing his glory (2:11, *etc.*).

itself unique. We have seen that Jewish healers and exorcists were not uncommon, and Jesus himself recognized the reality of their cures.[1] Besides, Jesus commissioned his own disciples to do the same kind of miracles that he did.[2] But the Gospels suggest that there was something strikingly unique about the simple, irresistible authority which Jesus showed, equally in the face of physical illness, demonic possession, and threats or shortages in the material world. It was not only, or primarily, *what* he did that impressed people, but *how* he did it.

Apart from the suggestion that he was using demonic powers, it was generally accepted that Jesus' power was derived from God. He himself argued that his exorcisms were proof that God was now taking decisive action against the powers of evil to set up his kingdom: 'It is . . . by means of God's power that I drive out demons, which proves that the Kingdom of God has already come to you.'[3] Mark records that exorcized demons recognized this too: 'What do you want with us, Jesus of Nazareth? Are you here to destroy us? I know who you are: you are God's holy messenger!'[4] This, then, was the day of God's victory. As the crowd at Nain put it after a spectacular miracle, 'God has come to save his people!'[5]

From this it was only a short step to the conclusion that Jesus was the Messiah, and again he himself led the way by using his healing miracles as proof of his Messiahship when John was in doubt.[6] The crowds agreed: 'Could he be the Son of David?' they asked after an exorcism.[7]

For all their recognition that it was the power of God that was responsible, his disciples soon began to realize that Jesus himself was someone rather special as well. 'Who is

[1] Lk. 9:49, 50; 11:19. [2] Mt. 10:8, *etc.*; see above, pp. 55, 56.
[3] Lk. 11:20–22; *cf.* 10:9. [4] Mk. 1:24; *cf.* Mk. 5:7; Lk. 4:41.
[5] Lk. 7:16; *cf.* 9:43. [6] Mt. 11:2–6.
[7] Mt. 12:23; *cf.* Jn. 7:31; 11:45–48.

this man?' they asked when he stopped the storm. 'Even the wind and the waves obey him!'[1]; and Matthew tells us that they even went so far then as to call him the Son of God.[2] Peter felt an almost superstitious awe when Jesus filled his nets with fish after a lean night, and begged him to go away.[3]

If Jesus did not normally perform his miracles as demonstrations, he certainly expected people to notice them, and to draw the right conclusions. His condemnation of the towns which gave him a cool reception was not so much because they rejected his teaching, but because even his miracles did not persuade them to repent and accept him; even the notoriously ungodly towns of Tyre, Sidon and Sodom, given such evidence, would have repented![4] This theme is taken up in the teaching of Jesus in John's Gospel: even if they were not convinced by his words, they should have accepted the evidence of his works that he was sent by God.[5]

So the Gospels suggest a cautiously balanced attitude to the significance of Jesus' miracles. They *are* evidence not only of the coming of God's day of victory, but also of the special position of Jesus himself as the one sent by God, the Messiah. The only proper response to them is to accept the authority of Jesus. But they are not by themselves a *sufficient* proof of who he is; indeed they are not primarily intended as a proof at all. They are only a part of the total picture of Jesus' ministry, only one aspect of the unique authority which Jesus displayed. Indeed they are far from being at the centre of Jesus' mission; he was very much more than just a miracle-worker. Faith based on his miracles alone would be too shallow: this is a regular

[1] Mk. 4:41. [2] Mt. 14:33.
[3] Lk. 5:8, 9. [4] Mt. 11:20–24.
[5] Jn. 5:36; 10:25, 32–38.

78

theme of the Fourth Gospel,[1] and it may well be the reason for his reticence in allowing the report of his miracles to spread too widely. He had more to accomplish than merely to go down in history as a nine-days' wonder.

---

[1] Jn. 2:23–25; 4:48; 6:26–29; 20:29.

6 Society

In the temple at Jerusalem stood thirteen containers shaped like trumpets, into which the faithful were invited to put their contributions for the upkeep of the temple and for charity. And contribute they did, on such a lavish scale that the temple, for all its extravagant regular expenditure, was still worth millions, and a law had to be passed to limit the size of donations! Men have never been reluctant to gain a reputation for generosity, and it seems there was little secrecy about the amounts rich men dropped in. Perhaps it was a regular attraction for spectators; certainly on one occasion Jesus and his disciples were sitting in the Court of the Women, watching the performance.

Among those who filed past the 'trumpets' was a poor widow. Presumably her clothes showed that she was a pauper, and made her conspicuous among the rich donors. Her contribution was two little bronze coins, the minimum donation permitted. And Jesus said, 'I tell you that this poor widow has really put in more than all the others. For the others offered their gifts from what they had to spare of their riches; but she, poor as she is, gave all she had to live on.'[1]

[1] Lk. 21:1-4.

That is typical of Jesus. He always seemed to take a delight in reversing the standards which most men accepted. One of his famous slogans was, 'The first shall be last and the last first.' He had no time for the barriers of convention and privilege which men erect between themselves to boost their self-importance. He was always the champion of the underdog.

So it was inevitable that in a society as rigidly structured along lines of class, race and wealth as our own, and further divided by the narrow Jewish definitions of religious orthodoxy and purity, Jesus should raise many eyebrows, even among his own disciples, and still more among the establishment. His disciples, eager to establish a proper pecking order among themselves, cannot have enjoyed his pronouncement that 'The greatest in the Kingdom of heaven is the one who humbles himself and becomes like this child'.[1] And when he told the story of the Pharisee and the tax-collector praying in the temple,[2] poking fun at the Pharisee's arrogant self-righteousness and concluding that the tax-collector, with his far inferior record of legal observance but also with a humble recognition of his failings, came off the better in the sight of God, any Pharisees in the audience must have been furious – and incredulous. Jesus' teaching simply turned accepted conventions upside down, and in so doing made him many enemies among those whose status he threatened.

Keeping doubtful company

But it was not only his teaching which gave offence. He practised what he preached.

Probably the most persistent and most serious cause for complaint was his habit of mixing with tax-collectors. Despised by Jewish patriots as collaborators with the

[1] Mt. 18:1–4.   [2] Lk. 18:9–14.

occupying power, rejected by the religiously orthodox as being mixed up with Gentiles, and hated by ordinary people for the excessive payments they demanded, the tax-collectors were virtually ostracized by the rest of Jewish society, and naturally tended to club together. The result was a sort of underworld of 'tax-collectors and sinners' with which a respectable Jew consorted at the risk of his reputation.

Among this group Jesus found a warm welcome, and an eager response to his preaching. One of them became a member of the Twelve. More than once we read of Jesus' presence at meals with tax-collectors (and sharing a meal was a symbol of particularly close identification), so much so that he achieved a reputation as 'a glutton and wine-drinker, . . . a friend of tax-collectors and outcasts'.[1]

Even in respectable company he could not be trusted. A dinner-party at a Pharisee's house was disrupted by a very unrespectable woman who came to find Jesus, and Jesus welcomed her. His host, naturally, was shocked.[2]

Jesus was unrepentant. He recognized in these outcasts of society a group who needed God's forgiveness, and who knew it. These were the people for whom he had a message. 'People who are well do not need a doctor,' he said when they criticized the company he kept, 'but only those who are sick. I have not come to call the respectable people, but the outcasts.'[3] It was this same criticism which evoked his three famous stories of the lost sheep, the lost coin and the lost son, which illustrate the joy which should greet the return of the lost.[4] But the religious authorities felt no joy, and certainly were not prepared to take a cue from people like this. So Jesus warned them, 'The tax-collectors and the prostitutes are going into the Kingdom of God

[1] Lk. 7:34.   [2] Lk. 7:36–50.   [3] Mk. 2:17.
[4] See Lk. 15:1–3 and following.

ahead of you.'[1] No wonder he was unpopular!

Even his disciples sometimes got irritated by the sort of people Jesus encouraged to come to him. Mothers brought their children to him, and Jesus refused to send them away.[2] A Gentile woman made a nuisance of herself clamouring for attention, and again Jesus would not ignore her.[3] On one occasion they arrived to find their leader in serious discussion with a Samaritan woman of dubious morals, and were rather shocked, though they knew him well enough not to voice their feelings.[4]

All these were women; one of the barriers Jesus seems to have refused to recognize was the 'male chauvinism' of his day. But even more significant is the fact that two of them were not even Jewish.

Gentiles

The barrier of race was more rigid even than those of class or sex or orthodoxy. Jewish theology consigned the Gentiles *en masse* to hell, and correct Jewish behaviour drew the logical conclusion and refused to have any more to do with them than the sad fact of a Gentile government demanded.

But here, too, Jesus refused to be restricted. Not that he spent much time, apparently, in non-Jewish company. His journeys outside Jewish territory were few and short. He recognized that his mission was essentially to 'the lost sheep of the people of Israel', and restricted his own activity and that of his disciples accordingly.[5] Few direct meetings with Gentiles are recorded, and on one of those occasions Jesus made a remark which suggested that Gentiles as such had a lower claim on his attention, though the sequel shows that this was more a test of sincerity than

[1] Mt. 21:31, 32. [2] Mk. 10:13–16. [3] Mt. 15:22–28.
[4] Jn. 4:27. [5] Mt. 10:5, 6; 15:24.

a real reluctance to help;[1] it is balanced by his declaration that the faith of the Gentile army officer was superior to any he had met in Israel.[2]

The point is that for Jesus race, like class, was irrelevant. It was *people* that mattered, people in need, people and their response to God. While he recognized the special status of Israel as the chosen people, and so made his appeal primarily to them, there was nothing exclusive about this. Indeed he agreed with John the Baptist that Jewish blood was no guarantee of the favour of God, and went even further: 'Many will come from the east and the west and sit down at the table in the Kingdom of heaven with Abraham, Isaac, and Jacob. But those who should be in the Kingdom will be thrown out into the darkness outside.'[3] Two of Jesus' parables make the same point uncomfortably clear.[4] Jesus was bad for Jewish national pride.[5]

Samaritans

The clear distinction between Jew and Gentile was blurred by the presence of the Samaritans, who occupied the territory between Galilee and Judaea. Very closely related to the Jews in race, language, and even religion, they had for centuries maintained a separate existence. Between the two communities there had built up that very special degree of mutual hatred which is reserved for those who are almost the same, but not quite. 'Jews', John tells us, 'will not use the same dishes that Samaritans use.'[6] While Jesus was a boy, Samaritans had desecrated the Jerusalem temple by scattering human bones in it at Passover time.[7] Jewish pilgrims from Galilee to Jerusalem could expect

[1] Mt. 15:21–28.   [2] Mt. 8:10.   [3] Mt. 8:11, 12.
[4] Mk. 12:1–12; Mt. 22:1–10.
[5] See further, below, pp. 103–105 and 121, 122, on Jesus' attitude to the special status of Israel.
[6] Jn. 4:9.   [7] Josephus, *Ant.* xviii. 2. 2 (29–30).

rough treatment in Samaria, and often took the long way round through Gentile territory across the Jordan to avoid trouble.

This is the background to Jesus' conversation with a Samaritan woman which so disturbed his (Jewish) disciples, but which resulted in a considerable following in Samaria, and even, incredibly, in an invitation to this Jewish traveller to stay with them, an invitation which was, of course, accepted.[1] Nor was this the only time they travelled through Samaria: once they met the usual cool reception, but Jesus refused the demand of James and John for retaliation;[2] on another journey Jesus cured a group of ten sufferers from leprosy, and was rewarded with the thanks of only one of them, a Samaritan![3] But the most daring affront to Jewish prejudice was the story, so well known that we have lost the point, of the Good Samaritan.[4] The point of the story is not the man's kindness, but his race. It is as if a white South African preacher used a black worker as an example to shame the pillars of the white establishment. Even a Samaritan can prove himself a true 'neighbour' (the word regularly used in the Old Testament for a fellow-*Israelite*) by his actions. Race is irrelevant. It is people that matter.

The Good Samaritan is a symbol of Jesus' own attitude, the immediate response to people in need, whether physical or spiritual, even if this meant crashing through conventional barriers.

Compassion

What are we to make of Jesus' attitude to Jewish society and its conventions? Was he one of those eccentrics who simply enjoys being unconventional, a natural non-

[1] Jn. 4:3–42. [2] Lk. 9:51–56. [3] Lk. 17:11–19.
[4] Lk. 10:29–37.

conformist? But on many points, as the next chapter will show, he conformed very properly. Was it the defiant challenge, born of an inferiority complex, of a Galilean in Judaean society? But most of the examples we have looked at have been set in Jesus' own Galilean environment. Was he, then, a convinced egalitarian, a sort of embryo Communist, deliberately setting out to abolish privilege and to tear down the framework of a class-structured society? But the interesting thing is that he does not seem to have attacked the social structure as such at all. He merely treated it as irrelevant when its conventions got in the way of higher claims. It was not the system which he attacked, but its *abuse* by those who used it to boost their own ego. It was not social structures, but *attitudes*, which Jesus condemned. It is those who 'make themselves great' who will be humbled;[1] it is the greedy and the gloating who are living in a fools' paradise.[2]

Jesus was interested in people, as people. Whether they were rich or poor, socially acceptable or 'not quite nice', male or female, Jew, Gentile or Samaritan, was of no importance. If they needed his help, he gave it; if they wanted God's forgiveness, he assured them of it. It was probably no surprise to him that it was among the underprivileged that he was most welcome; he was well aware of the dangers of pride and pomposity. But he went to the rich and powerful too, when they would accept him; he even had supporters in the Sanhedrin. Whoever they were, they were treated with a refreshing directness; no undue deference to the 'high', no condescension to the 'low', but all accepted simply as people.

A word which sums up Jesus' attitude is the good old-fashioned term, 'compassion'. The Greek verb refers literally to the entrails, which were regarded as the seat of

[1]Lk. 14:11; 18:14.   [2]Lk. 12:15–21.

emotion in the same way that we speak of the 'heart': we might paraphrase 'to be churned up inside'. Jesus was 'churned up inside' at the sight of a leper's deformity, of a widow's grief, of a crowd of people 'like sheep without a shepherd', of a crowd with nothing to eat.[1] Jesus was an emotional person. But his emotion was translated into action, and every time we hear of Jesus being 'churned up inside', we find him immediately taking steps to remedy the situation. In his parables too we find the same word used for the emotion of the Samaritan which made him break the racial taboo to help an injured man, and for the emotion of the Prodigal Son's father when the waster came home expecting humiliation and found instead a celebration feast.[2] Compassion leaves no room for conventional calculations and red tape. Jesus was a man of compassion, and so the barriers gave way.

Money

Probably the most serious social division, then as now, was the wealth gap. There are inequalities in any society which a man of compassion cannot ignore, and we can still catch the note of anger in Jesus' description of a callousness with which we are all too familiar: 'There was once a rich man who dressed in the most expensive clothes and lived in great luxury every day. There was also a poor man, named Lazarus, full of sores, who used to be brought to the rich man's door, hoping to fill himself with the bits of food that fell from the rich man's table. Even the dogs would come and lick his sores.'[3] Most of us in the affluent fraction of the world must wince.

What then was Jesus' attitude to money? What was his answer to the wealth gap?

[1] Mk. 1:41; Lk. 7:13; Mk. 6:34; 8:1, 2.
[2] Lk. 10:33; 15:20.   [3] Lk. 16:19–21.

'Jesus looked at his disciples and said:

> "Happy are you poor:
>   the Kingdom of God is yours!
> Happy are you who are hungry now:
>   you will be filled! ...
>
> But how terrible for you who are rich now:
>   you have had your easy life!
> How terrible for you who are full now:
>   you will go hungry!" '[1]

Some people try to spiritualize away the meaning of these words, in terms of humility and pride. But Jesus and his disciples *were* poor, and there is no reason to doubt that he meant just what he said. In their poverty they were far better off than the rich who had nothing to rely on but their money.

Jesus, as we have seen, came from a social group which, if not affluent, could be expected to have an adequate income. But his chosen style of life involved the loss of any financial security. He had no job, and no permanent home. 'Foxes have holes, and birds have nests,' he told a would-be disciple, 'but the Son of Man has no place to lie down and rest.'[2] He and his disciples lived on 'charity', on the contributions and hospitality of well-wishers.[3] He taught them to believe that God who could feed the birds could feed them too. Such money as they had they shared;[4] but there was no surplus left for anything beyond their basic needs.[5] They were certainly literally poor.

Once a rich man came to ask Jesus how he could achieve eternal life. Jesus very correctly listed off to him some of the Ten Commandments, but the man claimed, probably

[1] Lk. 6:20, 21, 24, 25.   [2] Lk. 9:58.
[3] Mt. 10:8–11; *cf*. Lk. 10:4–8; Lk. 8:3; 10:38–42; *etc*.
[4] Jn. 12:6; 13:29.   [5] Jn. 6:5–9; Mt. 17:27.

in all sincerity, that he had always kept them. Was that all he had to do ? 'You need only one thing,' Jesus replied. 'Go and sell all you have and give the money to the poor, and you will have riches in heaven; then come and follow me.' It was too much to ask, and Jesus lost a potential disciple.[1]

Was this then Jesus' formula, the renunciation of private possessions, a sharing out of wealth, an egalitarian society ? If this story were all the evidence we had, we might well think so. But it is not. Some of Jesus' followers were, and remained, rich and influential men.[2] Jesus' very dependence on hospitality demanded that some of his supporters kept their homes and their jobs. Even Peter, a constant member of Jesus' closest entourage, seems to have kept both his home and his boat and fishing gear, though he had little opportunity to use them during the period of Jesus' ministry.[3]

Then why did Jesus make this staggering demand of this one would-be disciple ? His remarks after the man had gone[4] do not suggest that he demanded poverty or renunciation for their own sake, but that it was a question of priorities. It is not necessarily wrong to be rich, but it can be dangerous. Money has a way of taking control of its owner, and it makes a tyrannous master; it can stop a man following the call of God. 'No one can be a slave to two masters . . . You cannot serve both God and money.'[5] And so Jesus had put to the rich man the highwayman's choice: your money or your (eternal) life. And he chose his money.

So it is a question of priorities. For Jesus, and therefore for his followers, God must come first. They could have

[1] Mk. 10:17–22.
[2] *E.g.* Nicodemus and Joseph, members of the Sanhedrin, who were able to bury Jesus at considerable expense in Joseph's own land (Jn. 19:38–42; *cf.* Mt. 27:59, 60).
[3] Mk. 1:29; Jn. 21:3.   [4] Mk. 10:23–31.   [5] Mt. 6:24.

money, but they must not worship it. Jesus' comments about rich people focus not on the fact of their wealth, but on their attitude to it and the way they use it. The devastating story of the rich fool[1] was provoked by an attempt to get him to adjudicate a family quarrel about a will. It was the greed which shocked him, the total selfishness and lust for money which still disfigures too many funerals, and leaves families irrevocably divided. The trouble with the rich fool was not that he had money, but that for him it was the be-all and the end-all. He hoarded it. He gloated over it. It was his god. And it let him down.

Jesus' attitude was the opposite: put God first, and the money will take care of itself – or rather God will take care of it.[2]

And if you put God first, this is going to affect the way you use your money. Sometimes it will seem ridiculous to a materialistic society, as it horrified Jesus' contemporaries to see a woman 'wasting' a year's wages on a spontaneous act of devotion: a waste to them, but 'a fine and beautiful thing' to Jesus.[3]

Love and compassion do not calculate returns. 'If you lend only to those from whom you hope to get it back, why should you expect a blessing? Even sinners lend to sinners, to get back the same amount! No! Love your enemies, and do good to them; lend and expect nothing back.'[4] 'When you give a lunch or a dinner, do not invite your friends, or your brothers, or your relatives, or your rich neighbours – for they will invite you back and in this way you will be paid for what you did. When you give a feast, invite the poor, the crippled, the lame, and the blind, and you will be blessed; for they are not able to pay you back.'[5]

Here again Jesus is turning accepted standards and

[1] Lk. 12:16–21. [2] Mt. 6:33. [3] Mk. 14:3–9.
[4] Lk. 6:34, 35. [5] Lk. 14:12–14.

90

conventions upside down. If you have the love for God, and the unselfish compassion for those in need, that Jesus demanded, you are going to be very conspicuous in a materialistic society, as Jesus was.

Jesus' programme for society

But what does all this mean for a society divided by income-brackets? What was Jesus' programme for reform? We must say the same here as we said about his attitude to the class-structure. He had no programme, in the sense of a plan for changing the system. He does not give explicit support to either capitalism or socialism, or to any other -ism. But he warns them all that the basic fault does not lie in the system, but in the people who run it. It is men's attitudes as well as their environments which need to be changed. As long as material considerations take first place, it will be selfishness and greed that dictate the pattern of life, whatever the system. Jesus' programme is not to abolish the system with all its inequalities, but to make them irrelevant. He taught that 'a man's true life is not made up of the things he owns, no matter how rich he may be'.[1]

Two thousand years of history have not disproved his verdict. Schemes for social reform have come and gone, and there is probably less inequality now in many parts of the world than there has ever been. The followers of Jesus have been in the forefront of many reform movements, and they will continue to be, because true compassion cannot be content to deplore the suffering of the under-privileged, but must fight the unjust structure of society which allows it. But the best of systems still founders on man's basic selfishness, and greed will continue to be the guiding principle of society until we have learnt, with Jesus, to put first things first.

[1] Lk. 12:15.

7 Controversy

'Then the chief priests and the Jewish elders met together in the palace of Caiaphas, the High Priest, and made plans to arrest Jesus secretly and put him to death.'[1]

Those who know the story of Jesus are familiar with his confrontation with the religious establishment, and it no longer surprises them. But surely it is a remarkable fact that the guardians of the Law of God conceived such an implacable hatred for a popular preacher, who called men to a closer relationship with God and an unselfish love for their fellow-men, that in the end they would rather have a convicted murderer released than allow Jesus to go on preaching his 'good news'. Remarkable, that is, to those who do not know the history of the religious intolerance and persecution which have scarred the centuries since they crucified the embarrassing Rabbi from Galilee. Why did it have to happen?

Most of us are used to thinking of those who opposed and eventually destroyed Jesus as 'the Pharisees'. This is not quite fair. We have seen above[2] that the dominant

[1] Mt. 26:3, 4.
[2] Pp. 20, 21. There were in fact two main priestly families, the Sadducean family of Annas, and the Boethusians, who had held the High Priest's office under Herod and Archelaus, but had lost it to the house of Annas

group in the Sanhedrin, and therefore in the body which eventually did away with Jesus, was the Sadducees, and it would be a mistake to confuse this worldly aristocratic minority with the scrupulously religious Pharisees.[1] While most of the recorded controversies of Jesus are with the scribes and Pharisees, and are concerned with the legal niceties which were their special preserve, the conflict did not remain at that level alone. Both Jewish groups (and to reduce them to only two is still an oversimplification)[2] felt themselves threatened by Jesus in different ways, and so, while normally there was little love lost between them, they found it expedient to close ranks against this common threat. It is the aim of this chapter to explore the roots of the conflict which made such a dramatic climax inevitable.

The Rabbi of Galilee

It may not be irrelevant to notice first that both the priestly establishment and the majority of the Pharisees, particularly those who, as scribes, became members of the Sanhedrin, were Judaeans. In view of the disdain which Judaeans felt for the religious 'deviations' of Galilee, it was bound to be an uphill struggle for Jesus, however orthodox, to gain a favourable hearing. The slightest hint of inde-

---

under the Roman prefecture. The Boethusians are not mentioned as such in the Gospels, though they may be the 'Herodians' who occasionally appear, as their political ambitions were linked with the Herods, while the house of Annas owed its position to the prefects. The differences between the two groups were due to political rivalry rather than to any significant disagreement over religious principles. I am accordingly taking the liberty of lumping them together as 'Sadducees'.
[1] See above, pp. 24, 25.
[2] E.g. the 'elders', often mentioned in the Gospels, were a lay aristocracy with considerable power in the Sanhedrin, whose views, at least on political matters, would largely coincide with those of the priestly Sadducees. The 'scribes' were mostly Pharisees, but only a minority of Pharisees undertook the full training for 'ordination' as a scribe, so that the two cannot simply be equated. 'Lawyers' are occasionally mentioned, and are perhaps to be roughly equated with the scribes.

pendence of thought, and he could be sure of a very critical reception. To receive a rapturous welcome from Galilean crowds was not the best way to commend his teaching to the Jerusalem authorities.

But you do not normally hang a man for coming from the wrong part of the country! While Jesus' Galilean origin was undoubtedly a factor in the conflict, it was certainly not the decisive one.

It is true, too, that Jesus lacked the formal scribal education which in later times qualified a man for the title 'Rabbi'. But at that time the rules were not so rigid. Jesus was regularly addressed as 'Rabbi' or 'teacher', and not only by his own disciples. Like a qualified Rabbi, he collected a group of disciples, sat down to teach them, and at least in the early part of his ministry was invited to preach at the synagogue service. Much of his teaching is concerned with the sort of discussions about the Law and its application which were the staple diet of rabbinic debate: how to keep the Sabbath, what are the conditions for divorce, which is the greatest commandment, and so on. Many of his sayings are quite closely paralleled in rabbinic literature, both in their form and in their content. In short, despite his lack of formal qualification, Jesus seems to have presented himself, and to have been accepted, in the familiar role of a Rabbi. There is no ground here for conflict.

Like a good Rabbi, Jesus based all his teaching on the Jewish Scriptures, quoting them freely, and affirming their authority in the strongest terms.[1] And he practised what he preached. While there were differences of opinion about how the Old Testament law should be interpreted and applied, his life no less than his teaching was governed by its principles. At least in his basic stance on Scripture

[1] *E.g.* Mt. 5:17, 18; Lk. 16:17; Jn. 10:35.

there could be no cause for complaint against the orthodoxy of Jesus.

Legal traditions

But complaints there soon were because, when it came to the practical business of applying the Old Testament Law, Jesus refused to be bound by traditional interpretations. His reverence for the Old Testament itself is in striking contrast to his sublime disregard for the elaborate legal system which later Jewish tradition had woven round it. A good Rabbi would always justify his interpretation by quoting an earlier Rabbi, or preferably a whole string of them. Not so Jesus: as far as we know he never cited the opinion of another teacher, however venerable, outside the bounds of Scripture. He simply took the biblical text and expounded it with a sovereign '*I* say to you . . .'. And what he said was not always what a scribe would want to hear.

We have already seen how he was in the habit of keeping company which no respectable Rabbi, with his rigid standards of ritual purity, should keep. On one occasion the issue came to a head when a group of Pharisees and scribes from Jerusalem accused Jesus and his disciples of ignoring 'the teaching handed down by our ancestors' on the correct method of washing before meals. Jesus exploded: 'How right Isaiah was when he prophesied about you! You are hypocrites, just as he wrote:

"These people, says God, honour me with their words,
But their heart is really far away from me.
It is no use for them to worship me,
Because they teach man-made commandments as though
    they were God's rules!"

And Jesus said, "You put aside the commandment of God and obey the teachings of men." ' He went on to

95

explain that it is not what goes into a man (food) that makes him unclean, but what comes out of him (the wrong thoughts which are the root of wrong words and actions).[1]

Jesus was sailing rather close to the wind here. Mark understands him to be abolishing the whole Old Testament concept of unclean food,[2] and though he did not explicitly go so far, this is a natural deduction from what he said. What is quite clear is that he cared very little for such ritual niceties, and roundly condemned many of the scribal traditions as human rules, which they set up as an excuse for evading the far more serious demands of God in Scripture.

This 'laxity' towards ritual traditions, as the scribes naturally viewed it, comes out still more sharply in Jesus' idea of keeping the Sabbath.

The Sabbath

What precisely was meant by 'keeping the seventh day holy' was a fertile source of scribal debate. The Mishnah, finally compiled about AD 200 but made up of scribal traditions stretching back to well before the time of Jesus, contains two long sections laying down in incredible detail just what is or is not permitted on the Sabbath. Thirty-nine classes of forbidden work had been identified,[3] but that is only the beginning, and the subdivisions and qualifications are legion. A broken limb may not be set; you may not cut your finger-nails, or search your clothes for fleas; it is disputed whether a cripple may take his wooden leg out of the house. Writing more than one letter is forbidden, unless you write with fruit-juice, dust or sand, which leave no lasting mark. A bucket may be tied to a belt but not to a rope. If fire breaks out, it may not be put out, and you may rescue only enough food for three meals, and as

[1] Mk. 7:1–23.   [2] Mk. 7:19.   [3] Mishnah, *Shabbath* 7:2.

many clothes as you can wear (not carry); you may, however, rescue all copies of Scripture.[1] A brief selection like this can give no idea of the complexity of the argument, covering every conceivable circumstance, what sort of knots may be tied, how far anything may be thrown, where on the person anything may be carried, and so on. As the Mishnah itself comments, 'The rules about the Sabbath are as a mountain hanging by a hair, for Scripture is scanty, and the rules many'![2]

It is hardly surprising that Jesus, who treated scribal ideas of ritual purity so lightly, was also impatient of this sort of casuistry. Not that he ever questioned the Old Testament command to keep one day holy; it was on the whole approach to *how* it was to be kept holy that they crossed swords.

The first clash was over his disciples' action in plucking and rubbing ears of corn in their hands to get the grain out to eat on the Sabbath: this constitutes reaping and thresh-ing, two of the thirty-nine forbidden acts. That they were hungry did not enter into the Pharisees' calculations; it was illegal. Jesus defended their action on two grounds. Firstly he claimed that 'the Sabbath was made for the good of man; man was not made for the Sabbath'; it was in-tended to be a blessing, not a burden. Secondly, and this must have enraged the Pharisees even more, he calmly asserted his own authority to lay down the interpretation of the Sabbath law. David had put human need before ritual niceties, and now Jesus claimed a similar authority: 'So the Son of Man is Lord even of the Sabbath.'[3]

Later clashes over Sabbath regulations (and five are recorded) are all concerned with Jesus' practice of healing

---

[1] These instances are all taken from Mishnah, *Shabbath*, from the following passages: 22:6; 10:6; 1:3; 6:8; 12:3–5; 15:2; 16:1–4.
[2] Mishnah, *Ḥagigah* 1:8.   [3] Mk. 2:23–28.

sickness when he met it, even if it happened to be the Sabbath. Again there is no hint of an apology, but the same appeal to a true sense of priority: 'What does our Law allow us to do on the Sabbath? To help, or to harm? To save a man's life, or to destroy it?'[1] The Mishnah does in fact allow medical care on the Sabbath if, and only if, there is actual danger to life.[2] But Jesus went beyond that, and healed any who came on the Sabbath. He went on to point out the inconsistency of their own standards: 'What if one of you has a sheep and it falls into a deep hole on the Sabbath? Will you not take hold of it and lift it out? And a man is worth much more than a sheep!'[3] In fact later Rabbis debated this very point. Some felt it was permissible to throw pillows and bedding into the pit, and if the animal could then climb out, well and good. Others said it should be fed, to keep it alive until it could be lifted out on a weekday. But the talmudic passage concludes (and it was presumably to some such argument in Jesus' day that he was referring) that since the avoidance of animal suffering is a biblical principle, it should override rabbinic rules[4] – they would waive the rules for animals, but not, apparently, for men!

Luke tells us that 'his answer made all his enemies ashamed of themselves, while all the people rejoiced over every wonderful thing that he did'.[5] No-one enjoys being humiliated in public, especially by one whom they regard as a danger to public morals. Jesus was adding insult to injury, and personal revenge was added to righteous indignation as a motive for silencing him.

Jesus the radical

We have seen that the root of this conflict of Jesus with the

[1] Mk. 3:4.   [2] Mishnah, *Yoma* 8:6.
[3] Mt. 12:11, 12. *Cf.* Lk. 13:15, 16; Jn. 7:21–24 for similar arguments.
[4] Babylonian Talmud, *Shabbath* 128b.   [5] Lk. 13:17.

scribes over interpretation of the Law was his refusal to bow to any authority other than the Old Testament itself. Matthew has preserved for us a series of six sayings where Jesus quoted what 'men were told in the past', and followed it by his own sovereign 'But now I tell you . . .'.[1] While in most of these cases what he quotes is a passage from the Old Testament, or something like it, his aim was not so much to set aside the Old Testament laws which he quotes as to show how the scribes were interpreting them without regard to the more general ethical principles of the Old Testament. Moses' insistence that divorce, once properly enacted, must be permanent[2] was being treated by some teachers as a justification for divorce for quite trivial causes.[3] His statement of the principle of proportionate legal retribution ('An eye for an eye and a tooth for a tooth') was taken as a licence for personal revenge; and the command to 'love your neighbour' (*i.e.*, fellow-Israelite) had been popularly expanded to include 'hate your enemy', which is nowhere to be found in the Old Testament.[4] Jesus' interpretations reject these convenient distortions, and go back to first principles. Similarly he insists that the Old Testament prohibitions of murder and adultery should not be taken purely literally and left at that, but that the spirit behind them must be taken into account: hatred is in principle no different from murder, and lust no different from adultery.

It is this 'radical' approach to the Old Testament which is responsible for Jesus' conflict with scribal orthodoxy. It

[1] Mt. 5:21–48.
[2] Deuteronomy 24:1–4. The wording quoted by Jesus is not quite what the original passage actually says.
[3] See further on this question Mk. 10:2–12.
[4] The Qumran sect had certainly already made this addition. Their members were taught to 'love all that God has chosen and hate all that he has rejected', to 'love all the sons of light and hate all the sons of darkness' (1QS 1:3, 4, 9, 10).

is not radical in the sense of being destructive, but in the true sense of the word, going to the roots of the matter, looking for the true spirit and intention of Scripture, and refusing to be content with a merely literalistic legalism. His question was not how much (or how little) am I obliged to do, but how can I most fully please God. He was neither simply a rigorist nor a libertine: on divorce he found the scribes too lenient, but on the Sabbath and ritual purity too rigid. His only concern was to interpret the Old Testament truly as a guide to the will of God, and in relation to men's real needs and concerns, not to bolster a man-made system.

Typical of Jesus' radical approach is his reply to a sincere question on a stock subject of scribal debate, 'Which commandment is the most important of all ?' He replied by quoting two texts, the commands to love God with all your heart, and to love your neighbour as yourself.[1] Both texts were very familiar, and indeed the famous Rabbi Akiba used the second in just the same way a century later, while the first was recited daily by every good Jew. But as far as we know no other Rabbi brought them together like this to sum up the basic principles of Old Testament religion. But for Jesus love came first, and if it meant bending, or simply discarding, the rules worked out by scribal tradition, so be it. This is the same 'compassion' we have noticed in previous chapters: people are the object of God's concern, so people come before rules. It was for people that the Old Testament had been written, and it must be with regard to people that it is interpreted. 'The Sabbath was made for man, not man for the Sabbath.'

It is not difficult to see why this attitude of Jesus led to conflict. The parched old wineskins of scribal tradition could not cope with the effervescent power of Jesus'

[1] Mk. 12:28–34.

radical interpretation of the Law.[1] It was bound to break out. In the event it looks rather as though it was the scribal authorities who made the break, for while Jesus seems to have been a welcome preacher in the synagogues at the beginning of his ministry,[2] we soon hear no more of this, and Jesus teaches the crowds out in the open. It looks as if he was thrown out.

'Hypocrites'

Theoretically, all this could have been discussed in a spirit of gentlemanly academic debate. Men can differ over points of interpretation without indulging in personal attack; indeed that is the way we feel religious debate ought to be conducted nowadays.

But it did not work out like that. We have already seen how Jesus was accused of being in league with the Devil, and how he in turn called his opponents 'hypocrites'. In fact we have not seen the half of it. 'Blind guides', he called them, and 'an evil and adulterous generation'. Among other choice epithets are 'snakes, vipers' brood' and 'sons of hell'.[3]

Jesus was too warm-blooded a person to be coldly academic. He can never be accused of ivory-tower theology. He lived among ordinary people, and when he saw the effect of scribal legalism on the man in the street, their complacent self-righteousness horrified him. Compassion spilt over into anger.

'Hypocrite' was his favourite word for them. Literally it means an actor, and Jesus accused the scribes and Pharisees of putting on a show of piety which was sadly at variance with their real character. They stood and prayed on street

[1] Mk. 2:21, 22.   [2] Mk. 1:21, 39; 6:2; Lk. 4:16–27.
[3] Mt. 23:16; 12:39; 23:33; 23:15; cf. his accusation that they were 'sons of the Devil' in Jn. 8:44.

corners, had a fanfare sounded when they gave alms, and put on a 'lean and hungry look' to draw attention to their fasting; 'they love the best places at feasts and the reserved seats in the synagogues; they love to be greeted with respect in the market places and have people call them "Teacher".'[1]

All this would not be so bad if they really deserved that respect. But in fact it was all superficial. 'You are like whitewashed tombs, which look fine on the outside, but are full of dead men's bones and rotten stuff on the inside.'[2] They were careful to separate off the correct proportion of their garden herbs for the temple offering, but forgot the primary obligations of justice, mercy and honesty.[3] They were quick to criticize other people's failings, especially in ritual matters, but blind to their own. In a playful sketch from the carpenter's workshop, Jesus pictures a man offering to take a speck of dust out of his workmate's eye when there is a big piece of wood in his own![4]

If it were only a matter of exhibitionism and a censorious attitude to the less fastidious, that would be bad enough. But Jesus' accusations do not stop there. The imposition of their petty regulations was a serious burden on the backs of ordinary people, and one which they, in the splendid isolation of their superior holiness, did nothing to help with. Not content with debarring themselves from a true relationship with God by their lop-sided legalism, they effectively debarred others too.[5] Further, Jesus accused them of using their reputation for piety to defraud gullible women.[6]

The use of smear tactics in political and even religious debate is familiar enough to us. But this is more serious.

[1] Mt. 6:2, 5, 16; 23:5-7; cf. the parable of the Pharisee's prayer, Lk. 18:11, 12.
[2] Mt. 23:27; cf. verses 25, 26.
[3] Mt. 23:23, 24.   [4] Mt. 7:3-5.
[5] Mt. 23:4, 13.   [6] Mk. 12:40.

While there was much in the teaching of the scribes which Jesus had to oppose, much more sinister was their whole attitude and approach to religion. Pompousness and censoriousness might be overlooked, but a fanatical devotion to legal minutiae combined with a complete unconcern for people added up to a very dangerous compound which Jesus could not ignore. It cut right across the 'good news of the Kingdom of God' which he had come to tell, and so he had to break out of the confines of academic debate and denounce them not only for what they taught, but for what they were.

Rocking the boat

Not surprisingly, then, Jesus had the enmity of the Pharisaic section of the establishment to reckon with. But it was not the Pharisees who eventually had the decisive voice in Jesus' death, but the chief priests and elders, the Sadducean group. It cannot have distressed them very much to hear Jesus denouncing the Pharisees as hypocrites. They might even have enjoyed it. What was it, then, that brought the Sadducean element into the fray?

Their concern was the preservation of the *status quo*; their own survival depended on it. Jesus' main crime in their eyes was that he started rocking the boat.

One day he told a story about a vineyard let out to tenants, who refused to pay the owner the share of the vintage which was due as rent, and beat up and killed those who were sent to collect it. Anyone who knew the book of Isaiah would recognize the allusion to Isaiah's song about Israel as God's vineyard.[1] 'What, then, will the owner of the vineyard do?' asked Jesus. 'He will come and kill those men and turn over the vineyard to other tenants.' The message was obvious, and 'the Jewish leaders tried to arrest

[1] Isaiah 5:1–7.

Jesus, because they knew that he had told this parable against them'.[1]

Other parables went further, and seemed to suggest that not only the Jewish leaders, but the nation as a whole, were ripe for punishment and rejection.[2] We have seen that Jesus talked of Gentiles coming into the Kingdom of God;[3] that was bad enough, but he went further and added the other side of the coin, the rejection of the Jews from the Kingdom which they regarded as their exclusive right. They had refused to listen to his appeal for repentance, and they must take the consequences.[4]

Jesus focused this grim message in his prediction of the destruction of Jerusalem itself, the holy city of the Jews, and the very heart of their national existence. His warning that not a single stone of the temple would be left in place[5] led on to a long discourse in which the coming destruction of the city is predicted in some detail.[6] Luke records three other occasions when Jesus warned them of what was going to happen to Jerusalem, once weeping openly when he saw the city in front of him and knew that his final appeal would be too late.[7]

Forty years later it all happened: the Romans under Titus destroyed the city so thoroughly that hardly any sections of Herod's magnificent temple have been discovered intact. To the Romans, no doubt, it was a necessary police action to restore order in a troublesome little province. But to Jesus it was far more: it was a long withheld punishment, the work of God himself. 'These

[1] Mk. 12:1-12.   [2] Lk. 13:6-9; 14:15-24.
[3] See above, p. 84.   [4] Mt. 11:20-24; 12:38-42.   [5] Mk. 13:2.
[6] It is disputed how much of the discourse recorded in Mark 13, Matthew 24 and Luke 21 refers to the destruction of Jerusalem, and how much to Jesus' second coming. Few would doubt, however, that such passages as Mk. 13:14-20, and especially Lk. 21:20-24 do in fact refer to the destruction of the city. Further details are added in Lk. 19:43, 44.   [7] Lk. 13:34, 35; 19:41-44; 23:27-31.

are "The Days of Punishment," to make come true all that the Scriptures say.'[1] Prophet after prophet had been silenced and murdered: 'I tell you indeed: the punishment for all these will fall upon the people of this day!'[2] And then Jesus had come, to offer them a last chance of repentance, to gather the people together 'as a hen gathers her chicks under her wings', and they were rejecting him too. So now the sentence must at last be carried out, 'because you did not recognize the time when God came to save you!'[3]

This stark message of rejection had its positive counterpart, as we shall see in the next chapter, but it takes little psychological expertise to see why the chief priests and elders were drawn into the fray, and soon took the lead in hunting Jesus down. Whatever you thought of his theology, this was inflammatory and treasonable stuff, and could not be ignored.

There was good reason, then, for Jesus to be removed. If you did not agree with him, you had to destroy him. He made neutrality impossible, as he always does.

The irony of the situation is that none of these were the charges actually brought against Jesus at his trials. He was charged first with blasphemy, on the basis of his claim to be Messiah and Son of God, and then with sedition, claiming to be the king of the very nation he had in fact threatened with destruction! But the formal charges were only the last stage in the process. The real reasons which united the Jewish authorities against Jesus were his threat to the religious system and self-esteem of the Pharisees, and to the political leadership and security of the Sadducees. He was dangerous, and so he was destroyed.

But they were too late. Less than half a century later the Sadducean establishment had vanished. Pharisaic Judaism survived, and still survives. But alongside it arose a move-

[1] Lk. 21:22.   [2] Mt. 23:29–36.   [3] Lk. 13:34, 35; 19:44.

ment far more powerful, and free to break out of the confines of the Jewish nation, a movement which put the love of God and man above the iron rules of conventional legalism, and which has brought men of all races to know God for themselves, through the Rabbi of Galilee.

8 The Kingdom

They once tried to make Jesus king – and he ran away. The incident brings into focus a question which has been in the background of all we have so far discussed, the most important question of all. We have talked about his dedication to his mission: what *was* his mission? We have seen his demand for absolute loyalty. Loyalty to what? He talked about 'the Kingdom'. What sort of kingdom, if he refused the crown when it was offered him? Unless we can answer these questions, we might as well be studying any idealistic reformer in history. What was so special about Jesus?

Jesus and Jewish liberation

Mark tells us that Jesus began his preaching in Galilee with the message, 'The right time has come, and the Kingdom of God is near!'[1] In view of what we saw in chapter 2 of the excitable state of Jewish feelings, especially in Galilee, and the growth of very definite hopes of political deliverance, it would have been surprising if such language had

[1] Mk. 1:15. Both Greek verbs are in the perfect tense ('has come near' rather than 'is coming near'), suggesting that the new state of affairs is not only imminent, but already present.

not led many to the conclusion that here at last was the Messiah, the Son of David, who had come to lead them to victory over the occupying forces. 'Kingdom of God' to a population with strong Zealot sympathies could hardly mean anything else. And it was on this charge that Jesus was eventually brought before the Roman prefect: 'We caught this man misleading our people, telling them not to pay taxes to the Emperor and claiming that he himself is Christ, a king.'[1] The official charge-sheet nailed to his cross labelled him sarcastically as 'King of the Jews'. Still today there are some who take this sort of language at its face-value, and conclude that Jesus was a political agitator for Jewish independence, a forerunner of the Zealots.

Jesus' enthusiastic reception in the early days in Galilee was no doubt due, at least in part, to such hopes. The fact that one of the Twelve was a 'Zealot'[2] may be significant, though the fact that he was prepared to make common cause with a tax-collector shows that it was not primarily for political reasons that he joined the movement. At least one of Jesus' disciples seems to have abandoned his hopes of national deliverance only when Jesus' death sealed his 'failure',[3] and even after his resurrection his closest followers had not yet given up the idea that he would 'give the Kingdom back to Israel'.[4]

---

[1] Lk. 23:2.

[2] Lk. 6:15, using the Greek term *zēlōtēs*. Matthew and Mark give the name *Cananaios*, which reflects the Aramaic term for a Zealot, *qan'ana'*. At the time of Jesus these were not yet technical terms for the political party (see above, p. 23, note 1), but they had become so around the time the Gospels were written, so the evangelists' use of them suggests that they knew that Simon, while not a member of an organized party, shared to some degree the ideals of the later Zealots. The original source of Simon's nickname may have been rather his active zeal for God's law. (Paul calls himself a *zēlōtēs* in this sense: Acts 22:3–5; Galatians 1:14; Philippians 3:6.)

[3] Lk. 24:21.   [4] Acts 1:6.

But the matter had already come to a head in the incident which seems to have marked a turning-point in Jesus' career.[1] Trying to escape for a time from the pressure of the crowds who were mobbing him in Galilee, he had taken the inner circle of his disciples across the lake to a lonely region for a 'retreat'. But the plan had leaked out, and they found themselves confronted by a large crowd of eager followers, running into thousands, who had tracked them down and who, not content with a further ration of teaching, seemed determined not to go away even though there was neither food nor housing available, and it was getting late.

Why this extraordinary persistence? They could hear Jesus preaching any time in Galilee, without going to such lengths to disrupt his plans for a well-earned rest. But the sequel suggests that their motive was more than a hunger for sermons. Mark tells us that they confronted Jesus 'like sheep without a shepherd', and that phrase is used in the Old Testament for an army without a commander.[2] John makes it clear that there was a political flavour to this gathering. For when Jesus met the immediate practical need for food by a miracle, their response, thinking no doubt of Moses (the great liberator) and his provision of manna, and of the current hope of the coming of a prophet like Moses, was to conclude, 'Surely this is the Prophet who was to come to the world!' Consequently, 'they were about to come and get him and make him king by force.'[3]

Such popular movements do not spring up in an hour or two. The best explanation for the persistence of this large crowd in pursuing Jesus into this remote area is that they had already decided that he was the leader they needed,

---

[1] The incident is recorded in all four Gospels. See Mk. 6:30-45, and for additional details Jn. 6:1-15.
[2] 1 Kings 22:17; cf. Numbers 27:17.   [3] Jn. 6:14, 15.

and were determined to force his hand. They had not left home for a sermon, but to launch a popular uprising, with Jesus as Commander-in-Chief.[1]

Jesus had no such idea. John says that, aware of their intention, 'he went off again to the hills by himself'. Mark adds the interesting note that 'at once Jesus made his disciples get into the boat and go ahead of him to Bethsaida, on the other side of the lake, while he sent the crowd away'. Were the disciples perhaps also infected with the patriotic enthusiasm of the crowd, that Jesus felt it necessary to pack them off in such a hurry ? At any rate, Jesus seems to have seen the situation as a serious threat, and to have lost no time in dissociating himself from the political designs of the crowd.[2] From this point on Jesus kept more out of the public eye, and concentrated on the private teaching of his disciples. He did not want to risk a repetition.

John goes on to tell us that after this 'many of his followers turned back and would not go with him any more'.[3] Jesus' failure to accept the 'Messianic' role he was offered would naturally disappoint the more politically minded among his followers, and a thinning of the ranks, at least of those prepared to join him on a full-time basis, would be inevitable. But it seems that the people in general did not yet give up hope that Jesus might be persuaded to launch an independence movement. When eventually he advanced on Jerusalem in a deliberately staged 'Messianic' gesture, all the old enthusiasm revived, and they shouted,

[1] For another insurrectionary movement originating in the desert see Acts 21:38 (with a comparable 'army' of 4,000); cf. Josephus, B.J. ii. 13. 5 (261–263). Other such movements are referred to by Josephus, Ant. xx. 5. 1. (97); xx. 8. 6 (167–168). He mentions that leaders of such groups were known as 'kings', Ant. xvii. 10. 8 (285).
[2] A variant reading in Jn. 6:15 has it that Jesus 'fled' into the hills. In as much as this is not the sort of language later generations of Christians would be likely to invent about Jesus, it may well be the original reading.
[3] Jn. 6:66.

'Praise to David's Son! God bless the king who comes in the name of the Lord!'[1] But again they were disappointed, and as the week wore on they realized that he still did not share their nationalistic ideals. Before the week was out, they were prepared to let him be executed.

Politics: human and divine

The fact remains that it was on a charge of political sedition that Jesus was executed. Very likely the tumultuous scenes on his final arrival in Jerusalem lent colour to the accusation. But the Roman prefect, we are told, found Jesus not guilty on this charge, and only signed the death-warrant under duress. And the evidence of the Gospels strongly supports his verdict.

It was a shrewd test of Jesus' political stance when his opponents put to him the question, 'Is it against our Law to pay taxes to the Roman Emperor? Should we pay them, or not?'[2] It was a loaded question, because it was on precisely this point that Judas of Galilee had based his revolt some twenty-five years earlier, saying that to pay taxes was no less than slavery, and treachery to God, the true king of Israel. It was from this revolt that the Zealot movement drew its inspiration. The question was, therefore, a clear test of Jesus' sympathy with Zealot ideals.

His famous answer, 'Pay to the Emperor what belongs to him, and pay to God what belongs to God', was not so evasive as is sometimes thought. It is preceded by the demand, 'Bring a *denarius*, and let me see it.' The denarius was the standard silver coin issued by the Roman authorities, and required for the payment of taxes. It carried a portrait of the Emperor. But the Romans were aware of Jewish scruples about 'graven images', and bronze coins

[1] Mt. 21:9; Lk. 19:38. See further, below, pp. 128–130, on this incident.
[2] The incident is narrated in Mk. 12:13–17.

were minted for use in Palestine which bore no portrait. A strict Jew had no need, therefore, to defile himself by using idolatrous imperial money.[1] The fact that Jesus' questioners were able to produce a denarius cut the ground from under their feet: they were using Caesar's money, so they could have no ground for refusing to pay his taxes with it.

Jesus' main intention, then, is to show up the disingenuous nature of the question. But no nationalist could have said, 'Pay to the Emperor what belongs to him,' and suggested that this was compatible with a prior obligation to God. Jesus' answer was not that of a total collaborator, but it was certainly not that of a Zealot.

But Jesus was hailed as 'Messiah'. Does this not inevitably brand him as a revolutionary? We shall be considering soon just what Jesus' idea of Messiahship was, but we may note here that Jesus seldom, if ever, referred to himself as 'Christ' (Messiah), and when others did so, while he did not deny it, he went on immediately to substitute his favourite title 'Son of Man', and to stress the non-political nature of his mission.[2] Even more obviously, he never called himself 'Son of David', or encouraged others to do so, and once he went out of his way to dissociate his idea of Messiahship from the title 'Son of David' with its political overtones.[3]

On one occasion he did engage in the sort of violent action one might expect of a revolutionary, but its target was not the Roman occupying forces, but the commercial

---

[1] The denarius represented a day's wage for a labourer, and so was a considerable sum. To carry on daily business without it, using only the smaller bronze coins, would therefore not be impossible; probably no more inconvenient than to live in Britain today without five-pound notes.
[2] See especially Mk. 8:29–33; also Mk. 14:61, 62. See below, pp. 116, 117.
[3] Mk. 12:35–37.

market which the religious leaders had allowed to grow up in the temple courtyard.[1] Generally, he was conspicuously opposed to violence.[2] His advice to 'turn the other cheek' is famous, but it is not so often noticed that he also gave the parallel illustration, 'If any one forces you to go one mile, go with him two miles.'[3] The Greek word for 'force to go' is the term for the Roman soldiers' practice of 'requisition-ing' labour, such as porters for carrying their equipment.[4] So Jesus' principle of non-retaliation to provocation went so far as to include compliance with the oppressive demands of the occupying forces. Finally, when one of his followers tried to put up armed resistance to prevent his arrest, Jesus soundly rebuked him.[5]

But perhaps the decisive evidence that Jesus was not the nationalist leader many of his followers wanted him to be lies in his declared attitude to the Jewish nation of his day. We have seen in the last chapter that he repeatedly asserted that his nation was destined for punishment and destruc-tion, not for triumphant independence. He talked of a Kingdom, to be sure, but we shall see shortly that that Kingdom had nothing to do with the chauvinistic ambitions

[1] Mk. 11:15–17. On this incident see further, below, pp. 130–132.
[2] The obscure words in Mt. 11:12 about violent men who try to seize the Kingdom of God should perhaps be interpreted as a repudiation of Zealot-type revolutionaries.
[3] Mt. 5:41.
[4] The same word is used for the soldiers forcing Simon of Cyrene to carry Jesus' cross, Mk. 15:21.
[5] Mt. 26:51–54. Many different explanations have been given of the strange episode about the swords in Lk. 22:35–38, ranging from the completely spiritualizing (that Jesus was merely warning them graphic-ally that life was going to be dangerous, and when they took him literally he corrected them with 'Enough of that') to the very literal (even in-cluding the suggestion of R. Eisler, adopted by S. G. F. Brandon, *Jesus and the Zealots* (Manchester University Press, 1967), p. 341, that they meant they had two swords *each*!). Any fair interpretation must take into account both the fact that they had at least one sword with them at the time of the arrest (Mk. 14:47), and also Jesus' protest that there was no need to send an armed force to arrest him as if he were a brigand (Mk. 14:48).

of the Jewish freedom fighters. A man who could talk freely to Samaritans and Gentiles and sit at table with quisling tax-collectors, and at the same time talk about Jews being excluded from the Kingdom and Jerusalem itself being reduced to rubble, was not even remotely in sympathy with Zealot ideals. Unless we are to accuse the Gospels of wholesale falsification,[1] we must accept that Jesus was not politically motivated, and found the nationalistic tendencies of his supporters acutely embarrassing. It looks as though we must give up the image of the political Jesus.

The man who fits no formula

When we try to discover what Jesus' view of his own mission really was, we soon discover that he is 'the man who fits no formula'.[2] None of the recognized Messianic[3] titles of his day was remotely adequate to express what he had come to do, just as we find that, if we try to confine him within one of our own modern Messianic titles (freedom fighter, social reformer, avant-garde theologian, guru, or whatever), we only make it more obvious that he is a unique figure. Some of the titles may be correct; none can be adequate. His own title for himself was 'Son of Man', and while his contemporaries seem to have recognized that there was some Messianic flavour about this name,[4] it was

[1] This is the view especially of S. G. F. Brandon, *Jesus and the Zealots*.
[2] This is the title of chapter 2 of E. Schweizer, *Jesus* (SCM Press, 1971), in which he examines the evidence of the Gospels.
[3] The terms 'Messiah' and 'Messianic' are used throughout this chapter in the general sense of the one through whom God was to fulfil his Old Testament promises (see above, p. 22), not with specific reference to the use of the actual title Messiah (Christ), except where the context indicates this.
[4] It was derived principally from Daniel 7:13, a passage which all Jewish interpreters took as a Messianic prophecy. On the origin and significance of the term see further my *Jesus and the Old Testament* (Tyndale Press, 1971), especially pp. 136–138.

not in current use as a Messianic title, and it left them puzzled.[1] Other more recognized titles he used hardly at all, and seems to have discouraged others from using them about him.

So if we are to understand what Jesus was trying to do, we must beware of being tied down to any one title or idea, and try to do equal justice to the many different strands in his teaching about himself and about the Kingdom of God, even when they do not fit easily into a tidy scheme. Ultimately we shall find that the only true answer to the question 'Who is Jesus?' is not a cut-and-dried formula, but a personal confession.

The Messiah

'The time is fulfilled' was the manifesto on which Jesus launched his Galilean ministry. This note of the fulfilment of all that the Old Testament had looked forward to characterizes much of what he had to say about his mission. 'Many prophets and kings,' he told his disciples, 'wanted to see what you see, but they could not, and to hear what you hear, but they did not.'[2] John the Baptist wanted to know if Jesus really was 'the coming one', and Jesus replied by pointing to the way some key Old Testament prophecies were being literally fulfilled in his ministry.[3] Many other such allusions are scattered throughout his teaching; they refer both to well-known Messianic passages and to quite obscure details, but all of them Jesus sees as pointing forward to his own mission, and finding their fulfilment in him.

Given this sort of language, it is hardly surprising that eventually his disciples came to think of him as the Messiah.

---

[1] See especially Jn. 12:34.   [2] Lk. 10:24.
[3] Mt. 11:3–5. Jesus' reply is drawn from the words of Isaiah 35:5, 6 and 61:1, with possible allusions also to Isaiah 26:19 and 29:18, 19.

Even people outside the group had begun to talk about him as 'the Prophet', and in a day in which prophecy as the Old Testament knew it was regarded as extinct, this could only mean the one great prophet like Moses who was popularly expected by both Jews and Samaritans to usher in the 'day of the Lord'.[1] But while the idea that Jesus was the Messiah had probably been growing in the disciples' minds for some time, it did not come out into the open until the period after Jesus had refused the overtures of the nationalist movement and withdrawn from the public eye. As they were travelling together in the north, on the slopes of Mount Hermon, Jesus put the challenge to them, 'Who do you say I am?' And Peter answered simply, 'You are the Messiah.'[2]

Jesus did not deny it. It would have been strange, in view of all his claims to be fulfilling the expectations of the Old Testament, if he had. But Mark tells us that he immediately swore them to secrecy. Even more significantly, he immediately dropped the title 'Messiah' in favour of his own term 'Son of Man', and began to say things about his mission as Son of Man which were the very opposite to what 'Messiah' would conjure up in a Jewish mind. He began to teach them that the Son of Man must suffer, be rejected by the authorities, and eventually be executed. It was too much for Peter, who had just voiced the conviction that Jesus was the Messiah, and no doubt looked forward to the honour of being his right-hand man in his triumphant career. He took Jesus aside and remonstrated with him. But Jesus was not one to compromise, and Peter, whose ideas were really only typical of Jewish

[1] The expectation was based on Deuteronomy 18:15–18. Jn. 6:14 clearly refers to this expectation, and Mt. 21:11; Lk. 7:16 point the same way. Jesus occasionally referred to himself as a prophet: Mk. 6:4; Lk. 13:33.
[2] Mk. 8:27–30.

expectation, had to take the stinging rebuke, 'Get away from me, Satan. Your thoughts are men's thoughts, not God's!'[1]

Why did Jesus feel so strongly about this? It gradually becomes clear as the story evolves towards its climax at the cross that his ultimate suffering and death was not for Jesus the regrettable by-product of his refusal to compromise, but was itself the very heart of his mission. He had, as he said, come to give his life. This idea of his 'Messianic' role was so totally foreign to most current Jewish thought, that Jesus found he had to insist on it more and more firmly as the climax approached, to prevent his disciples giving way to the very natural temptation to look for an easier way. That was why Peter's well-meant advice produced such a sharp reaction.

Death and glory

Starting from this crucial revelation at Caesarea Philippi, Mark records three formal predictions by Jesus of his coming suffering and death;[2] but to look at these alone is to miss the remarkably persistent way this theme crops up in his teaching on many different occasions, ranging from incidental allusions to deliberate theological teaching about his mission.[3] He said not only that he would, but that he *must* suffer, and this because it was laid down for him in Scripture. So while he did not actually, as far as our sources go, talk explicitly of suffering and death as the proper role of 'the Messiah', it would be hard to understand his recorded words any other way.

What he did do was to refer unmistakably on a few

[1] Mk. 8:31-33.   [2] Mk. 8:31; 9:31; 10:33, 34.
[3] A study of the following passages will give some impression of the persistence of the idea: Mk. 2:20; 9:12; 10:38, 45; 12:6-8; 14:8, 21-25, 49; Mt. 26:54; Lk. 9:31; 12:50; 13:32, 33; 17:25; 22:37; Jn. 7:19, 33, 34; 10:11-15; 12:23-25; *etc.*

occasions to one particular Old Testament passage, the fifty-third chapter of Isaiah, which portrays the 'Servant of the Lord' who suffers and dies on behalf of the people of God, 'by whose stripes we are healed.' It is a passage which seems to have caused some embarrassment to orthodox Jews, who recognized it as a portrait of the Messiah, but could not come to terms with the idea that the Messiah could be anything but a conquering figure.[1] But what for most Jews was a puzzle proved to be for Jesus one of the clearest outlines of his mission, and there can be little doubt that it was this passage above all others which moulded his conviction that 'the Son of Man must suffer'.[2]

In two significant sayings based on this passage he makes it clear that he expected his suffering to be for the benefit of others: his death would set them free as a ransom frees a captive.[3] In the light of Isaiah 53, it is clear what sort of freedom he had in mind, for that passage speaks of the Servant of the Lord being 'wounded for our transgressions', 'bruised for our iniquities', 'numbered with the transgressors', and 'bearing the sin of many', with the result that he will 'make many to be accounted righteous'. This is not a question of political freedom achieved by martyrdom, but of spiritual release of the sinner, accomplished by the death in his place of the sinless Servant of the Lord.

But Jesus' conviction that he must suffer and die did not finish there, for interwoven with his predictions of 'defeat' from Caesarea Philippi on is the certainty of vindication.

[1] The Aramaic Targum (paraphrase) of this chapter systematically transfers every reference to suffering from the Servant to the wicked, or to Israel as a whole; it is quoted in full in W. Zimmerli and J. Jeremias, *The Servant of God*[2] (SCM Press, 1965), pp. 69–71. The same book (pp. 37–79) gives a full discussion of other early Jewish interpretations of Isaiah 53.
[2] This is disputed by a few recent scholars. See the full discussion in my *Jesus and the Old Testament*, pp. 110–132.
[3] Mk. 10:45; 14:24.

All the three formal announcements of his coming suffering in Mark end with the declaration that after his death 'he will be raised to life'. Alongside Isaiah 53, his other favourite Old Testament passage in this connection was Daniel 7, particularly the vision in verses 13, 14 of the coming of 'one like a son of man' to receive an everlasting kingship, the passage from which, apparently, he derived his favourite title 'Son of Man'.[1] These two great Old Testament prophecies fused together in his mind to produce the certainty that his mission was first to suffer and die for the sins of men, and then, raised from that death, to be triumphantly vindicated by God and become the acknowledged ruler of all men for ever.

It was with such a conception of his mission in mind that Jesus set out for Jerusalem, knowing quite well that it would be to his death. He remarked ironically that 'it is not right for a prophet to be killed anywhere except in Jerusalem'.[2] He had no illusions, and did not allow his disciples to have any. Mark paints a striking picture of Jesus striding purposefully ahead on the road to Jerusalem, his disciples following 'filled with alarm', while a larger crowd behind them were simply scared.[3] He was a man with a mission, and he was determined to get on with it.[4]

Reconciliation and forgiveness

So Jesus set out to die. But what did he hope to achieve by it? We have ruled out political liberation as his aim, and he does not seem to have wanted to reform the social system. Undoubtedly he had a great deal of ethical teaching to offer, but that is hardly adequate to explain his determined march to death. What *was* his aim, which demanded such ruthless self-sacrifice?

[1] Jesus clearly alludes to these verses in Mk. 8:38; 13:26; 14:62; Mt. 19:28; 25:31; 28:18.
[2] Lk. 13:33.   [3] Mk. 10:32.   [4] Lk. 12:50.

In a word, he wanted to reconcile men with God.

Words like 'sin', 'iniquity', 'transgression' leave most of us cold these days, but it was common ground among the Old Testament writers and no less among the Jews of Jesus' day that man's relationship with God depended on his willingness to give his first loyalty to God, and not to go his own way (which is what 'sin' means in the Bible). The recurrent problem of Old Testament Israel had been its rebellion against God, and it was still this thought which was uppermost when John the Baptist came appealing for repentance before the judgment of God fell on them, and calling them to 'a baptism of repentance for the forgiveness of sins'. It was this same problem which Jesus, inspired particularly by Isaiah 53, set out to deal with.

Ideally he would have liked to see his nation as a whole return to its true loyalty to God. But the attitude of the religious establishment soon made it clear that they had no intention of repenting, indeed that they recognized no need for repentance. So Jesus turned increasingly to those who did accept that all was not well, and there he found the response he was looking for. In the house of Zacchaeus, a notoriously corrupt tax-collector, Jesus welcomed his change of heart as the true fulfilment of his mission, 'for the Son of Man came to seek and to save the lost.'[1] His reply when they criticized the company he kept makes it clear where his priorities lay: 'I have not come to call the righteous, but sinners to repentance.'[2]

Not that he had an exclusive interest in any one social or religious group. Anyone was welcome, provided he recognized his need for forgiveness and for a new relationship with God. And so gradually a new community began to emerge, a community of the forgiven. It was drawn from all classes, and even, as time went on, from Gentiles as well

[1] Lk. 19:10.   [2] Lk. 5:31, 32.

as Jews. The conventional barriers of human society were irrelevant.[1]

The true Israel

But Jesus never lost his concern for the salvation of Israel, the people of God. He would gladly have brought the whole Jewish nation back to their true state as God's people. But as it became clear that this was not going to happen, and that the Jewish nation in its present form was heading for destruction, not salvation,[2] he seems to have thought of the growing community of his followers as the true people of God, the 'Israel' in whom God's Old Testament promises to his people were to be fulfilled. The Jewish establishment by its rejection of his message was forfeiting its status, and the true Israel was now the narrower, and yet potentially far wider, community of the forgiven.

Not that he called them 'Israel', but there are many indications that this was his thought. His choice of twelve, the number of the founding fathers of the tribes of Israel, for the number of the inner circle of his disciples points this way.[3] Sometimes he referred to his disciples in terms used in the Old Testament for the nation of Israel, and he regarded several Old Testament passages about Israel as finding their fulfilment in this new community.[4]

From this standpoint he could envisage men from all corners of the earth coming to join the patriarchs of Israel at the heavenly banquet, while the 'sons of the Kingdom' found themselves outside.[5] It was no longer the descendants of Abraham as such who would constitute the true Israel, but all those, Jew or Gentile, who showed by their repent-

[1] See above, pp. 80–85.
[2] See above, pp. 103, 104, for Jesus' predictions of this destruction.
[3] See especially Lk. 22:30 for the connection.
[4] See my *Jesus and the Old Testament*, especially pp. 60–67.
[5] Mt. 8:11, 12.

ance and by their acceptance of Jesus' message that they really were the people of God. For the present, most of them were in fact drawn from the old Israel, but the people of God could no longer be confined to a single race. Israel was being reborn.[1]

The centrality of Jesus

In all this, Jesus was not just the prophet of the new community. He was in a much fuller sense its founder. He not only called men to a new relationship with God, but he saw his own suffering and death as the key to that relationship. As the Servant of the Lord he would 'pour out his soul to death' and be 'numbered with the transgressors', and so he would 'make many to be accounted righteous, and bear their iniquities'.[2] Old Testament religion had found in its sacrificial system the way to cure the estrangement between men and God which was the inevitable result of sin: now the one great self-sacrifice of Jesus, 'as a ransom for many,' would provide the permanent solution to the problem. Without it there could be no community of the forgiven.

And this new community, this true expression of the Old Testament ideal of Israel, was not only Jesus' creation: it was an extension of himself. In a sense he *was* the true Israel, embodying in himself all that Israel should have been, and was not. The figure of the Servant of the Lord in Isaiah 53, and the 'one like a son of man' in Daniel 7, were both in their original intention not only, or even primarily, individuals, but representations of the ideal people of God, and it was in these figures above all that Jesus saw his mission foreshadowed. Similarly we have seen how in his confrontation with Satan after his baptism

[1] See C. H. Dodd, *The Founder of Christianity* (Collins, 1971), chapter 5, for a clear and balanced discussion of this aspect of Jesus' mission.
[2] See Isaiah 53:11, 12.

Jesus grounded his resistance to Satan's suggestions on the analogy between Israel's wilderness experiences and his own, and proved to be the true Son of God in a way Israel had failed to be.[1] Nor was this the only time Jesus presented himself as fulfilling Old Testament passages relating to Israel as a people.[2]

In a culture where the individual is all-important, this sort of thinking is hard to grasp. But the oriental world in which Jesus lived found no difficulty in seeing a group embodied in an individual, a nation in its king, an army in its general, or a family in its head. So Jesus himself was Israel, and in him the hopes and promises of Old Testament Israel found their fulfilment. The status of his disciples as the true people of God was theirs not because of what they were in themselves, but because they were his. Jesus himself was the key to the new relationship with God to which he summoned men. That was what he had come for.

The Kingdom of God

I headed this chapter 'The Kingdom', and began by saying that the arrival of 'the Kingdom of God' was at the centre of Jesus' preaching. Since then, I have barely used the term at all. This was deliberate, because most people have only the vaguest idea of what 'the Kingdom of God' might mean, and so I have tried to explain in other words how Jesus understood his mission. Now, in the light of what we have found, what did he mean by 'the Kingdom of God'?[3]

'Kingdom' really suggests all the wrong ideas. It makes us think of a place, or at least of a group of people: the

[1] See above, pp. 41, 42.
[2] For details see my *Jesus and the Old Testament*, pp. 50–60.
[3] There is no difference in meaning between 'Kingdom of heaven' and 'Kingdom of God', the former being the expression preferred by Matthew, the latter by other New Testament writers.

kingdom of Nepal, or the United Kingdom. But the New Testament word is a more abstract one; it refers not to a place but to a state of affairs, the situation in which God is king. It would be better represented in English by 'reign' or 'rule' or 'sovereignty'. Further, 'kingdom' is a political term, but we have seen very clearly that Jesus was not interested in gaining political power. The Kingdom of God is not a new system of government. Wherever God is in control, his sovereignty accepted and his will obeyed, there is the Kingdom of God. Ideally the Kingdom of God means that all men everywhere acknowledge God. But when even one man submits to God's claims on him, there in essence the Kingdom of God has already come. He has, to use Jesus' own language, entered the Kingdom of God.

So when Jesus announced the coming of the Kingdom of God, he was declaring that it was his mission to restore the relationship of men with God. As one after another accepted his teaching and submitted to God as Lord, so the Kingdom of God began to become a reality. In the community of the forgiven which Jesus founded, the Kingdom had come.

Of course there is a sense in which the Kingdom of God cannot really be said to have come until *all* men come to recognize the sovereignty of God, and he is undisputed King of all mankind. There is a strong note in Jesus' teaching of looking forward to 'the coming of the Kingdom' in that sense. And in that sense the Kingdom still has not come, and still we must pray 'Thy Kingdom come', until God's will is done on earth as it is in heaven, when Jesus himself returns in glory, the Son of Man to whom 'was given dominion and glory and kingdom, . . . an everlasting dominion, which shall not pass away'.[1]

But that ultimate ideal should not blind us to the very

[1] Daniel 7:14.

vital sense in which we can already say, 'Thine *is* the Kingdom.' For much of the Kingdom-language in Jesus' teaching relates not to that ultimate consummation, but to the Kingdom as it was already being seen, as the powers of evil fled in disarray,[1] and men and women found themselves brought through the ministry of Jesus into a right relationship with God. That was the Kingdom Jesus came to establish, a Kingdom 'not of this world',[2] but with an effect on life in this world which no political revolution could dream of, a Kingdom which could not be held by the narrow limits of the Jewish nation, and which will only be fully established when all men everywhere gladly acknowledge the sovereignty of God.

[1] For this aspect of the coming of the Kingdom see Lk. 10:18; 11:20.
[2] See Jn. 18:33-37.

9 Confrontation

The Passover festival at Jerusalem in the days before the temple was destroyed was an impressive occasion. Perhaps the only comparable event in the modern world is the annual Haj to Mecca. From all over the Eastern Mediterranean world, wherever Jews had settled or foreigners had embraced the Jewish religion, they came each year. Nobody knows exactly how many came. Ancient reports range from half a million to twelve million! A more conservative modern estimate reckons that Jerusalem, quite a small town by modern standards (perhaps 30,000 inhabitants), was swollen to six times its normal population at Passover time.[1] The city itself could not hold them, and they filled the surrounding villages, while large numbers set up tents outside the city.

Last visit to Jerusalem

It is at Passover time, probably the third Passover of Jesus' public activity,[2] that we return to a chronological account of Jesus' life. Much has happened since the early days when

[1] J. Jeremias, *Jerusalem in the Time of Jesus* (SCM Press, 1969), pp. 77–84.
[2] See above, p. 45, note 2.

he joined John the Baptist in the Jordan valley, an un-known village carpenter. Now he is famous, or notorious, depending on your point of view. Over the last two years or so the character of his mission has gradually become clearer, at least to those closest to him, and the lines are now drawn for the final confrontation with the establishment. Jesus himself has no illusions about the outcome: he has come to die, 'to give his life as a ransom for many'. And so he has come to Jerusalem, for 'it is not right for a prophet to be killed anywhere except in Jerusalem'.[1]

He was expected. A good week before the Passover the pilgrims would begin to gather at Jerusalem, to carry out the necessary rites of purification before the festival, and also, no doubt, to be sure of finding a place to stay. John tells us that 'they were looking for Jesus, and as they gathered in the Temple they asked one another, "What do you think? Surely he will not come to the feast, will he?"' Not if he valued his life, certainly, because the authorities were ready for him, and had plans to arrest him and dispose of him if he showed up.[2]

Prudence would have dictated that Jesus should lie low at least during the sensitive period of the festival. In this particular year the atmosphere was likely to be even more highly charged than usual, for some sort of patriotic rising had been crushed recently enough for some of its leaders to be still in prison awaiting execution.[3] The authorities would have had reason to keep a careful watch, even without the arrival of a Galilean preacher with a record of attracting enthusiastic crowds.

And yet he came. Of course the Law demanded the presence of every able-bodied Jewish man at the festival; but many found little difficulty in evading the requirement for far less cogent reasons than a threat to their lives. But

[1] Lk. 13:33.   [2] Jn. 11:55–57.   [3] Mk. 15:7.

Jesus had to come. He had a message to deliver, a challenge to present to his nation, and what better time to present it than the Passover, when so many Jews were together in one place? Besides, if, as he was well aware, his mission was to lead to his death, there was a special appropriateness in the Passover season, when the killing of the Passover lambs reminded them how God had once protected his people from destruction through the blood of lambs, when he brought the Israelite slaves out of Egypt to be the people of God.

The dramatic entry to Jerusalem

Jesus came to Jerusalem from the east, by the Jericho road. He had with him probably quite a large group of his disciples, and other Passover pilgrims from Galilee and the Jordan area would be coming in by the same road, as this was the peak time of arrival for the festival. Among this crowd Jesus could probably have arrived unnoticed, if he had wanted to, as he had done at a previous festival.[1] But this time there was no point in concealment: he had come to be noticed.

So he staged a deliberately dramatic entry into the city.[2] The approach to Jerusalem from the east is barred by the low ridge known as the Mount of Olives, separated from the city by the deep little valley of the Kidron. Somewhere in the Bethany region, on the east side of the ridge and still out of sight of the city, Jesus borrowed a donkey.

It looks as if this was pre-arranged, as the disciples sent to collect the animal were given it without hesitation when they repeated the 'password', 'The Master needs it.' Presumably the owners of the donkey were supporters of Jesus; we know of at least one house in Bethany at which

[1] Jn. 7:10-14.
[2] Mk. 11:1-10. Further details in Lk. 19:28-40 and Jn. 12:12-19.

he was a welcome visitor.[1]

But why borrow a donkey? It can hardly have been because Jesus was tired of walking: he had walked all the way from Galilee, and had barely three miles to go! Moreover, there is no other record of Jesus travelling except on foot.

It was a symbolic act, with a clear message to a Jew who knew his Scriptures. He might have thought of King David, riding out over the Mount of Olives on a donkey when his son tried to seize his throne, and returning by the same way to his capital in a peaceful triumph.[2] But his first thought would surely be of Zechariah's message of hope to Jerusalem:

> 'Lo, your king comes to you;
>   triumphant and victorious is he,
>   humble and riding on an ass,
>   on a colt the foal of an ass.'

The passage goes on to describe how military hardware would be abolished, and 'he shall command peace to the nations'.[3]

So Jesus was, quite clearly, presenting himself as Jerusalem's long-awaited king, David's successor, the Messiah. But it is typical of him that the method he chose of making the claim was in stark contrast with what most Jews expected of their Messiah; no pomp and pageantry, no war-horse at the head of an army to expel the Romans, but a humble donkey, a crowd of festival pilgrims, and a king of peace.

His followers could hardly miss the point, and neither apparently did the other pilgrims on the road. They put out the red carpet (in the form of clothes and greenery

Lk. 10:38–42; Jn. 11:1–5; 12:1–9.   [2] 2 Samuel 15:30; 16:1, 2.
[3] Zechariah 9:9, 10.

strewn on the road), and turned the pilgrim's arrival into a triumphal procession. 'Praise God! God bless him who comes in the name of the Lord! God bless the coming kingdom of our father David! Praise be to God!'[1]

All this could have been done in the spirit of Zechariah's prophecy, and of Jesus' non-political idea of Messiahship, but the reference to the kingdom of David is sailing rather close to the wind of popular militancy. And as other demonstrators came out of the city to meet the procession, it must have seemed to many Galilean pilgrims as if their earlier hopes of Jesus as a nationalist leader were at last to be fulfilled.

The demonstration in the temple

So Jesus' arrival in Jerusalem, although planned to stake his claim to a non-military Messianic role, was not likely to allay the suspicions of the authorities, already on edge after the previous rising.

The sequel was worse.

The first place a pilgrim would make for when he arrived would be the temple. Entering the spacious outer court (the 'Court of the Gentiles')[2] he would find a large crowd of pilgrims and, in the shaded colonnades along the sides of the court, a thriving market in sacrificial animals. It was obviously convenient for the worshippers to be able to buy the animals they needed on the spot, though no doubt at suitably inflated prices, and the priests in charge of the temple encouraged the traders to come there. It was also obligatory to use the special Tyrian coinage for temple offerings, and so money-changers set up their stalls for the

[1] Mk. 11:9, 10.
[2] 'Court' perhaps suggests an outer section of the temple building itself. It was in fact a vast walled area, about six times the size of Trafalgar Square, within which the temple building stood. The traders were thus in the temple precincts, but not in the building itself.

convenience of the pilgrims, and also no doubt for their own substantial profit on the transactions.

Into this busy and noisy scene Jesus strode, and instantly caused havoc. He 'began to drive out all those who bought and sold in the Temple. He overturned the tables of the money-changers and the stools of those who sold pigeons, and would not let anyone carry anything through the Temple courts.'[1] The Gospel accounts suggest that Jesus acted alone, and that he carried all before him. Certainly he cannot have had much active help or met with serious resistance, or the Roman garrison, whose fort overlooked the Court of the Gentiles and who would be on the alert for trouble during the festival period, would surely have intervened. It seems that Jesus' sheer personal authority stunned the traders into submission. Before the authorities could intervene, it was a *fait accompli*.

Jesus' action is often seen as a spontaneous outburst of anger at the misuse of his Father's house. Certainly his accusation that they were turning the house of prayer into a robbers' cave shows his anger at the desecration of a holy place. But it was not quite spontaneous. Mark mentions that on Jesus' first arrival in the temple he merely 'looked round at everything'; it was on the next day that he acted. The demonstration was apparently planned overnight, and was as deliberate a gesture as the donkey-ride into Jerusalem.

And there was more to it than an attempt to abolish

[1] Mk. 11:15, 16. John places this incident at the opening of Jesus' ministry (2:14ff.), and it is not certain in which chronological context it fits better. I am here following the Synoptic order, because such a deliberate confrontation with the authorities, with clear Messianic overtones, seems more probable at this final stage of his ministry than in the very early days. It follows naturally from the provocative manner of Jesus' arrival, and contributes significantly to the animosity which brought about his trial and death. (It is sometimes argued, of course, that two similar incidents occurred at the beginning and end of Jesus' ministry, one recorded by John, the other by the Synoptics.)

commerce from the temple precincts. Jesus can hardly have expected that a single one-man demonstration, however impressive, would permanently break an established practice which enjoyed the support of the authorities. It was a gesture rather than an attempted reform.

As a gesture, it was breath-taking. It expressed at a stroke Jesus' total disapproval of Israel's religious leadership, which could allow the temple to be so misused. Trade had replaced worship, and it was no longer the house of God. It is not too much to read into Jesus' protest a demand for a whole new approach to the worship of God.

And his action gave more than a hint of his own role in this new development. The renewal of the temple was one of the blessings expected at the coming of the Messiah.[1] Two Old Testament passages in particular could hardly fail to come to mind. Malachi warns that 'the Lord whom you seek will suddenly come to his temple ... But who can endure the day of his coming, and who can stand when he appears? For he is like a refiner's fire, ... and he will purify the sons of Levi and refine them like gold and silver, till they present right offerings to the Lord.'[2] Even more pertinently, Zechariah had predicted that, when the day of the Lord arrived, 'there shall no longer be a trader in the house of the Lord of hosts on that day'.[3] So Jesus' action, like the manner of his arrival, is tantamount to a Messianic claim. As Messiah he sets himself above the priestly authorities of the temple, and carries out his Messianic function of purifying its worship.

[1] The visions of Ezekiel 40–48 already gave rise to such hopes, and they were fed by Zechariah 6:12, 13. A number of references in later Jewish writings testify that this hope was alive at the time of Jesus.
[2] Malachi 3:1–3.
[3] Zechariah 14:21 (RSV). Some older versions read 'Canaanite' for 'trader'. The same Hebrew word bears both meanings, but it is now generally agreed that the racial meaning would be irrelevant in the context. The Aramaic Targum adopts the meaning 'trader'.

Preliminary skirmishes

Such an act of defiance could not be allowed to pass. Jesus had thrown down the gauntlet publicly, and the authorities had to take it up. The Gospels now show Jesus caught up in a series of public debates with both priestly and Pharisaic leaders. They challenged his right to act as he had done, and probed his stance on various key issues of scribal debate, ranging from theoretical questions about life after death to the very practical and explosive issue of Roman taxation.[1] Couched as academic debates, these questions were in fact not nearly so innocuous. They were collecting evidence against him, hoping for blasphemous claims about his own status which would count against him in a trial before the Sanhedrin, or for Messianic language which would give plausible support to a charge of sedition before the Roman governor. If he avoided incriminating himself in either of these ways, he could hardly fail to damn himself in the eyes of his popular following, who were more than ready to use Messianic language about him, and would not take kindly to any apparent weakening of his stand. They could hardly lose.

Jesus handled the delicate situation with all the skill of a politician. He avoided the clear-cut answers which would have played into their hands, sometimes manoeuvring his opponents into answering their own questions. But, unlike many politicians, he did more than play with words. Without making incriminating claims, he succeeded in implying that he, like John the Baptist, was sent by God, and so had a right to act as he had done, and that his Messiahship was something far higher than the nationalistic 'son-of-David' ideology,[2] as well as getting across some significant practical and theological teaching.[3] The few

[1] See above, pp. 111, 112. [2] Mk. 11:29–33; 12:35–37.
[3] Mk. 12:13–17, 18–27, 28–34.

encounters specifically recorded in the Gospels are no doubt only a sample from what must have been a fascinating running dialogue during the days leading up to the festival.

But for all Jesus' tactical skill in debate, he had no intention of softening his challenge to the religious leadership. It is in this setting that we find him telling his pointed story about the dishonest tenants who were thrown out of the vineyard.[1] It was a veiled threat, perhaps, but an unmistakable one. In a situation already so highly charged, such uncompromising language could have only one result.

Judas Iscariot

Meanwhile, Jesus' attention was not wholly occupied with the leaders. The presence of the pilgrims preparing for the Passover celebration provided a large and responsive audience, while the colonnades around the temple court formed a natural auditorium. Here Jesus taught during the day. What he taught the crowds at this stage we can only guess, as the Gospels concentrate on his debates with the authorities and his private teaching of his disciples during this period. But there is no reason to think that his popularity grew any less.

This posed a problem for the authorities. You cannot bring a man to trial without arresting him, and to try to arrest a popular teacher from the middle of a crowd of excited supporters could only lead to the very breach of the peace they were anxious to avoid. The answer was to arrest him at night. But this too posed a problem. Jesus, together with many of the pilgrims, did not have accommodation in Jerusalem. Each night he left the city, and disappeared into the anonymity of the Passover crowds camping in the neighbourhood. Luke tells us that he used

[1] See above, p. 103.

to spend the night on the Mount of Olives,[1] perhaps in the olive-orchard called Gethsemane to which he again retired on his last night.[2] To isolate Jesus' group at night among all the pilgrims camping on the hillside would have taken a very efficient police force – or an inside informer.

And that was where Judas came in. It must have seemed too good to be true when he volunteered to guide them to the place where Jesus could be arrested quietly at night. But Judas was genuine: for reasons which can only be guessed, he had decided to leave the sinking ship. A suitable reward was agreed, and Judas was committed to earning the title of the most famous traitor of all time.

Judas was well paid for his co-operation, and John tells us that he was more interested in money than was good for him.[3] But is even so considerable a sum as thirty shekels of silver[4] alone sufficient to make a man betray the cause into which he has invested some of the best years of his life? Few have thought so, and many other motives have been suggested.

If Judas was the only non-Galilean in the inner circle of Jesus' disciples,[5] he may not have found it easy to accept the leading position of the Galilean fishermen, Peter, James and John, and we may suspect an element of cultural pride combined with the jealousy of frustrated ambition.

But more probably it was with the essential character of the movement, not its personnel, that he had become

[1] Lk. 21:37.
[2] He stayed the first night in Bethany (Mt. 21:17; Mk. 11:11, 12), which was on the farther slope of the ridge, but later events suggest that Gethsemane was their regular site thereafter (see Lk. 22:39; Jn. 18:2).
[3] Jn. 12:6.
[4] This was equivalent to 120 denarii, and the denarius was an average day's wage for a labourer. The annual temple tax was only half a shekel per head.
[5] See above, pp. 53, 54.

disillusioned. If Judas, like so many of Jesus' followers, had hoped for a nationalistic liberation movement,[1] by this time it must have been clear to one so close to Jesus that this was not his intention. Jesus' talk of going to Jerusalem to die, and the certainty of a confrontation with the authorities, would then have convinced him that now was the time to get out before it was too late. It is even possible (and this is the most charitable explanation, if not the most probable!) that Judas had genuinely come round to the official point of view that Jesus was a false prophet and a blasphemer, so that he, like Saul of Tarsus a few years later,[2] regarded it as his clear duty to destroy him.

The motive is guesswork, but the fact is clear. The authorities had their inside informer, and there was nothing now to prevent their arresting Jesus, as they were anxious to do, before the Passover actually began.

The Last Supper

Time was getting short, and Jesus knew it. He and his disciples had come to Jerusalem for the Passover, but he knew it would be his last, and indeed things were now moving so fast that he might not live to see the festival begin. Yet he was anxious to hold a Passover meal with his closest followers before he died.[3] So the night before the ritual slaughter of the Passover lambs with which the festival proper began, Jesus presided over what was apparently an anticipation of the Passover meal.[4] Twenty-

[1] Some have seen his title 'Iscariot' as a corruption of 'Sicarius', the title of one of the most militant nationalist groups. But see above, p. 53, for the more probable derivation of 'Iscariot'.
[2] Acts 26:9–11.   [3] Lk. 22:15.
[4] John clearly dates the death of Jesus at the time the Passover lambs were killed, *i.e.* on the afternoon before the regular Passover meal. (Jn. 18:28; 19:14; *etc.*) This agrees with the Babylonian Talmud (*Sanhedrin* 43a) which says that Jesus was hanged 'on the eve of the Passover'. The Synoptic Gospels are generally taken to date the death of Jesus a day later. It is not always remembered, however, that the

four hours later, when other groups and families celebrated the festival at the proper time, Jesus was dead.

It was a farewell meal. But that is far too trivial a description of its significance. Like Jesus' entry to Jerusalem and the demonstration in the temple, it was deliberately symbolic.

Jewish day began at sunset, so that the slaughter of the lambs (beginning about 3 p.m.) was on the 'day' before the Passover meal eaten that evening after sunset. If the timing of the Jewish day is kept in mind, the Synoptic Gospels do not necessarily disagree with John's chronology, for if the Last Supper was prepared and eaten after sunset on the evening before the slaughter of the lambs, it was in fact on the same (Jewish) day, as Mk. 14:12 states, and the death of Jesus would then fall on the following afternoon, the time of the slaughter of the lambs. (Mk. 14:2 (= Mt. 26:5) may be a further indication that the Synoptics, like John, believed that Jesus was arrested before the festival proper began.) If this is so, the Last Supper could not be a full Passover meal, and it is striking confirmation of this that the eating of the lamb, the focal point of the Passover meal, is not mentioned in any of the Gospel accounts. Jesus called it a 'Passover' (Mk. 14:12, 14; Lk. 22:15), for such it was in intention, though circumstances made it necessary to hold it a day early, and without the lamb.

The whole question is too complex to be solved in a few lines. The following diagram, however, sets out the view of the chronology which I believe best accounts for the evidence of all four Gospels:

OUR CALENDAR		JEWISH CALENDAR	
	Sunset		
			NISAN 13
	Midnight		
THURSDAY			
	Sunset		
LAST SUPPER			NISAN 14
	Midnight		
FRIDAY		PASSOVER EVE	
CRUCIFIXION	*Noon*		
		Lambs slaughtered	
BURIAL	*Sunset*		
		Passover meal eaten	NISAN 15
	Midnight		
SATURDAY			
		SABBATH	
	Sunset		
			NISAN 16
	Midnight		
SUNDAY			
RESURRECTION			

The use of a guest-room in Jerusalem had been pre-arranged with a local supporter,[1] and the meal was made the occasion for some vital last instructions. John devotes five chapters of his Gospel[2] to the teaching Jesus gave at this meal, beginning with the symbolic act of washing his disciples' feet, going on to a great deal of teaching on what it would mean to be his disciple in a hostile world when he was gone, and concluding with the great prayer in which he committed them to God's keeping.

It was at this meal, too, that Jesus first revealed to the inner circle that it would be one of their own group who would betray him to the authorities. Judas' camouflage had been good, and even then the others could not guess which of them it would be. Jesus could have told them, and no doubt they would not have allowed Judas to leave the room. But Jesus gave only an indefinite identification, and Judas got away to set his plans in motion.[3] Not for the first or last time, Jesus passed over a chance to stop the course of events which was to lead to his death.

But the real focus of this last meal, the purpose for which it had been arranged, was reached when Jesus solemnly took bread and wine and offered them to his disciples in a symbolic gesture which has ever since formed the basis of the central act of Christian worship. He broke the bread, and offered it to them as his body, 'given for you'; he offered them the wine as his 'blood of the covenant, poured out for many'. And he told them to go on doing this 'in memory of me'.[4]

This is not the place to go into all that the Lord's Supper

[1] Mk. 14:12–16.   [2] Chapters 13–17.
[3] Mk. 14:17–21; Jn. 13:21–30. The host's act of giving a piece of food dipped in the common dish to a guest (Jn. 13:26) was apparently normal practice, and would take place frequently in the course of a meal.
[4] Among the many small variations in the wording of the records of this action (Mk. 14:22–24; Mt. 26:26–28; Lk. 22:17–20; 1 Corinthians 11:23–25) these central words seem to be firmly established.

can and should mean to the Christian who takes it seriously, still less to wade into the muddy waters of centuries of Christian conflict over the precise status of the bread and wine in the act of worship. But what did it mean to those eleven bewildered men who first heard these words on Passover Eve in Jerusalem?

First, and unmistakably, it put an end to any hopes that they may still have been clinging to that Jesus did not really mean what he said about coming to Jerusalem to die. He was symbolically enacting his death, which he knew was only hours away.

But it also explained why that death was necessary. The body given 'for you', and the blood poured out 'for many' point to the redemptive purpose of Jesus' death which he had already begun to teach them, and the words 'for the forgiveness of sins' in Matthew's version make the point more explicitly. He was not going to die for a cause, but for people, as the sacrifice which alone could bring them back to God.

At Passover time they could not miss the point. The Passover meal was a reminder of how God's people were rescued by the blood of the first Passover lambs. And that rescue had been the beginning of Israel as a nation, when they came together at Sinai and accepted God's covenant. Now Jesus' blood is 'blood of the covenant'; the new covenant is established by the sacrifice of Jesus, and Israel is reborn. From this night it is Jesus, the final perfect sacrifice, who is the foundation of the true people of God.

And this deeply significant act, he said, they were to continue to perform in his memory. The yearly reminder of the first Passover was to be transcended by the regular re-enactment of this simple visual aid, to remind them of this greater Passover when Jesus died for the sins of many, and the new covenant was made.

Centuries of debate were to follow, as Christians continued, and still continue, to 'do this', and to find deeper and deeper nuances of meaning in that simple act. But for those eleven men, this was quite enough to digest. It might be no bad thing if modern Christians could occasionally lay aside their accumulation of eucharistic theology, and recapture the ominous but revolutionary symbolism of Jesus' simple words and acts to those who first witnessed them.

Death, to most people, is final. It would be only natural if the disciples, engrossed by the now inescapable thought that Jesus was about to die, could see little immediate grounds for hope. But Jesus was already looking beyond the next twenty-four hours. 'I tell you,' he added after offering them the wine, 'I will never again drink this wine until the day I drink the new wine in the Kingdom of God.'[1] What was about to happen was not the end, but a new beginning. The Kingdom of God was becoming a reality. The future was not a funeral, but a feast.

Gethsemane

The eleven disciples no doubt left the guest-room with their minds in a whirl. They knew disaster was near, betrayal and death for their leader, and real danger, no doubt, for themselves. But if even a little of Jesus' meaning had sunk in, they must have known that something excitingly new was going to come of it, that they were caught up in one of the decisive moments of the history of God's dealings with men.

Jesus led them through the streets to the city gate, and down across the steep Kidron valley. Across the stream, they climbed the lower slopes of the Mount of Olives until they came to their regular rendezvous, the olive-orchard

[1] Mk. 14:25.

called Gethsemane (a name which means 'oil-press'). And there they stopped. It would have been easy to give the slip to Judas and the authorities by choosing a different place to spend the night, but again Jesus made no attempt to thwart their plans. He stayed in Gethsemane, a sitting target.

But for all his refusal to interfere with the course of events, Jesus was still appalled by the thought of his coming suffering and death. While the disciples, exhausted as much by their bewilderment and the sense of crisis as by the late hour, were soon asleep, Jesus went off by himself and prayed. 'Father! my Father! All things are possible for you. Take this cup away from me.' Mark tells us that he was in 'distress and anguish', almost crushed by sorrow.[1]

This is strong language for Mark, and many writers have speculated on why Jesus, who had so long predicted his suffering and death, and had come to Jerusalem specifically to die in fulfilment of his Messianic role, should be so appalled to find his predictions about to come true. It was to be a peculiarly horrible execution, certainly, far different from Socrates' painless draught of hemlock with which it is sometimes glibly compared; but few believe that that is enough to explain Jesus' revulsion. More likely it was the understanding that in his death he was to 'bear the sin of many', as 'the Lord laid on him the iniquity of us all',[2] that he could not bear. But whatever the reason (and it is presumptuous to imagine we could ever understand it), the prayer in Gethsemane rules out any suggestion that Jesus was a sort of demi-god, aloof from the emotions the rest of us share. The physical agony he was soon to experience was more than matched by the spiritual pain inflicted by his involvement with man's rebellion against his Father.

[1] Mk. 14:33–36.   [2] Isaiah 53:12, 6. See above, p. 118.

But stronger than both was his commitment to the work he had come to do, and his prayer finished with words which could be written large across his whole life: 'But not what I want, but what you want.' The issue had really been settled in his first confrontation with Satan after his baptism: there is no easy way out for the Son of God.

Then Judas arrived. He earned his money easily. Jesus made no attempt to hide or to escape, and the armed posse made short work of the pathetic efforts of eleven drowsy men to resist his capture. There is a gentle mockery in Jesus' reproach: 'Did you have to come with swords and clubs to capture me, as though I were an outlaw?'[1] Anything less like a band of desperadoes is hard to imagine.

The disciples saw there was no point in trying to rescue a man who seemed only too ready to be arrested. They melted away among the olive-trees.

Jesus was bound, and taken back into the city.

[1] Mk. 14:48.

10 Condemnation

It was Passover Eve. The morning was to bring the great day of the festival, when the lambs would be slaughtered in their thousands in the temple, and in the evening, as the Sabbath began, every Jew in the city would share in the ritual meal. Meanwhile, all over the city and on the hillsides around, the pilgrims slept.

But the chief religious authorities of the Jews had more important business in hand, and it was urgent, if they were to get Jesus safely out of the way before evening. Before noon the Gospels record no less than six examinations of Jesus by different authorities, of varying degrees of formality, and perhaps of legality. To talk about 'the trial' of Jesus is a drastic simplification of a complex series of hearings, the connection between which is not always clear. But the outcome is not in doubt – indeed it was probably not seriously in doubt from the start: before the evening, Jesus was dead.

First hearing: Annas
The first hearing was before Annas, to whose house John tells us that Jesus was taken immediately by the arrest party.[1] Annas had been High Priest until deposed by the

[1] Jn. 18:12–23.

Roman prefect some fifteen years before, to be succeeded after a short interval by his son-in-law, Caiaphas, who still held the office. But Annas was the head of the High Priestly family, and in many Jews' eyes he was still the true High Priest (as indeed the Gospels occasionally describe him). He seems to have been the moving force behind the clampdown on Jesus, and so it was to him that Jesus was first taken.

John records a short interrogation, but of course Annas had no official competence to try Jesus, and so in due course he was sent on to Caiaphas, whose office made him president of the Sanhedrin, the Jewish supreme court.[1]

Second and third hearings: the Sanhedrin

In Jewish eyes, Jesus' examination by the Sanhedrin was the 'real' trial. It was clearly right that an offence involving claims to a unique religious authority should come before the supreme religious tribunal of the Jews. The Roman authorities accepted this view, and had no interest in interfering in Jewish religious debates. In religious matters, the competence of the Sanhedrin was unchallenged and its verdict final.

The complication came from the Jewish law itself which prescribed the death penalty for certain serious religious offences, including blasphemy, the charge on which, as we shall see, Jesus was to be convicted. But the Romans kept to themselves the prerogative of carrying out capital punishment.[2] So if the death penalty was to be exacted, the

---

[1] See above, pp. 20, 21.
[2] This has been disputed, on the grounds of a few records of execution by the Jewish authorities in this period (*e.g.*, Stephen, Acts 7:54–60). It is generally accepted, however, that such cases were occasional illegal acts, lynchings rather than judicial sentences, which the Roman authorities might connive at, but did not officially permit. It was Roman policy throughout the Empire to deny capital powers to local authorities.

offender must be brought to a Roman court (in which, of course, blasphemy was not an admissible charge). This ambivalent situation accounts for some of the complexities of the trial of Jesus. To the Romans, the hearing before the Sanhedrin was an unofficial preliminary hearing, while to the Jews the Roman trial was a regrettable necessity to give effect to a sentence already passed, on other grounds, by themselves.

The Gospels tell us of two hearings before the Sanhedrin, one at night at Caiaphas' house, shortly after the arrest, the other early in the morning, presumably in the regular council chamber in the temple precincts.[1] It seems likely that the first was a less formal gathering, hastily summoned to prepare the charge for the formal session in the morning.[2] Mark gives details of the proceedings, leading to the vote for the death penalty, at the night hearing, while Luke gives a very similar account of the morning session. In the nature of the case the proceedings at the two meetings would need to cover much the same ground, and precisely when the verdict was formally given matters little.

Much is sometimes made of the supposed illegality of the Sanhedrin trial, in that the rules laid down in the Mishnah for capital cases do not seem to have been observed in several respects.[3] It is questionable, however,

[1] Mark (followed by Matthew) mentions both sessions (14:53ff.; 15:1). Luke gives details only of the morning session, but mentions that Jesus was taken to Caiaphas' house for the night (22:54ff., 66ff.). John says nothing about what happened to Jesus between his arrival at Caiaphas' house and his being taken from there to the governor in the morning (18:24–28).
[2] Mishnah, *Sanhedrin* 4:1, says that capital cases could only legally be tried in the daytime; it would in any case probably take several hours to gather the full Sanhedrin for a formal session.
[3] Mishnah, *Sanhedrin* 4–7. The following rules are often cited: capital trials must not be held on a feast-day or the day preceding; they must not be held at night (but see above); they must begin by hearing the case for the defence; and conviction must not take place the same day as the trial begins.

whether all these rules were in force at the time of Jesus. In any case, the fact that the legal conviction of Jesus was in the Roman court, not by the Sanhedrin, robs the argument of much practical significance.

More important than its technical legality is the atmosphere of the trial, held in great haste, to dispose quickly of a man whose removal had been planned for days. If a case for the defence had been presented, it is unlikely that it would have had a sympathetic hearing. The interval between the two hearings was spent by Jesus' Jewish guards in mocking and tormenting him, and the wording of the account suggests that even members of the Sanhedrin joined in the fun:[1] hardly a fair judicial atmosphere! It is hard to avoid the impression that the verdict was a foregone conclusion.

The Jewish verdict

Apart from the absence of a defence, however, the form of a legal trial seems to have been fairly carefully observed.[2] Various witnesses were called to substantiate charges, but under the stringent cross-examination which was insisted on in the rabbinic courts they failed to establish their testimony. One charge singled out in the Gospel accounts was Jesus' alleged threat to destroy the temple and build another in its place. This was very plausible, as Jesus had indeed predicted the destruction of the temple,[3] and this pessimistic, if not sacrilegious, strain in his teaching was a major cause of the hostility of the authorities. His recent one-man demonstration in the temple court would lend colour to the charge that he intended to destroy it himself, and a saying of Jesus dangerously like the alleged threat is

[1] Mk. 14:65.
[3] The following account is based on Mk. 14:55–64.
[2] See above, pp. 103, 104.

146

recorded elsewhere.[1] But this charge too failed under cross-examination.

Meanwhile Jesus himself apparently said nothing. There was, as yet, no case to answer. Besides, defence would probably have been futile in the loaded atmosphere, and might only have provided material for further charges. But in any case it would have been out of character for the man who refused to evade or resist arrest to intervene in the trial which was leading inevitably to the goal for which he had come to Jerusalem, and which he had accepted a few hours earlier as his Father's will.

This left Caiaphas in a difficult position. You cannot convict a man without reliable evidence, and so far the evidence had proved far from reliable. He decided on direct action. He left his seat[2] and stepped forward to confront Jesus with a direct question which he could not ignore: 'Are you the Messiah, the Son of the Blessed God?'

Caiaphas had been well briefed on Jesus' teaching and the things his followers were saying about him, and his blunt challenge at last broke through Jesus' silence. For all his reluctance to use such language in public, he could not evade such a plain question on the very basis of his mission. 'I am,' he replied.[3]

But he did not leave it at that. When Peter had first hailed Jesus as the Messiah, Jesus had immediately

---

[1] Jn. 2:19. The allegation persisted; see Mk. 15:29; Acts 6:14.
[2] The judges were normally seated. It was laid down that they should stand up after hearing evidence of blasphemy (Mishnah, *Sanhedrin* 7:5). If this convention dates back to the time of Jesus, was Caiaphas perhaps prejudging the issue by standing now?
[3] The wording in Matthew is less definite, literally '*You* have said' (*cf.* Lk. 22:70). This is not necessarily evasive, and is certainly not a denial: the subsequent verdict of blasphemy proves that. It is a qualification, accepting the substance of Caiaphas' phrase, but indicating that Jesus himself would have worded it differently: 'You could put it like that.'

substituted his favourite phrase 'Son of Man'.[1] Now, at this critical moment, he did the same thing, because he was not prepared to countenance the political ideas that clustered around the word 'Messiah'. But this was no retraction of his claim. Indeed if anything he made matters worse by adding, 'and you will all see the Son of Man seated at the right hand of the Almighty, and coming with the clouds of heaven!'

It was all Caiaphas needed, and he tore his clothes, as the judge was required to do when evidence of blasphemy was produced. Witnesses and cross-examination were not needed now: the judges themselves had heard the incriminating claim. The verdict was unanimous: Jesus was a blasphemer,[2] and the penalty for blasphemy was death.

And that, in Jewish eyes, was that.

The sentence could not be carried out, however, without the official sanction of the Roman prefect. And so Pontius Pilatus comes into the story which has made his name immortal.

To have come to Pilate with a charge of blasphemy would have been futile. But Caiaphas' tactics had paid off here too, for he had extracted a claim to be Messiah in front of the most unimpeachable witnesses, and a Messianic claim, coupled with Jesus' record as a popular hero and demonstrator, made good political ammunition. So Caiaphas stood to win all round. Blasphemy alone would have cut no ice with Rome, while a political charge alone would have made Jesus a patriotic martyr in the eyes of Jewish nation-

[1] See above, pp. 116, 117.
[2] The claim to be Messiah was probably not in itself technically blasphemous, but coupled with the claim to be Son of God, and to sit at God's right hand, it could hardly be allowed to pass – unless, of course, it was true! It has been suggested, too, that Jesus' reply 'I am' may have been taken as pronouncing the divine name (see Exodus 3:14), which was the technical definition of blasphemy at a later date (Mishnah, *Sanhedrin* 7:5).

alists. But here was good political material for Roman ears, while a conviction for blasphemy in the Jewish supreme court would ensure that Jesus was remembered, if he was remembered at all, not as a martyr but as a heretic.

Fourth and fifth hearings:
Pilate and Antipas

Early in the morning, then, Pilate was disturbed by a deputation of Jewish officials demanding instant execution of a dangerous nationalist leader.

He would not be surprised. No doubt he always came to Jerusalem at festival time prepared for trouble, and after the recent disturbances[1] he can hardly have expected this Passover to go off without incident.

At the same time, he would have had cause to be suspicious. The Sadducean leaders in the Sanhedrin were diplomatically subservient to Rome, certainly, but their zeal in denouncing a fellow-countryman as a rebel, when he had not even come to the notice of the occupying forces, must have rung rather hollow.

Besides, Pilate was not the sort of man to go along with Jewish demands without good reason, certainly not to be a mere rubber stamp on their independent decisions. He is described by a contemporary as 'naturally inflexible, a blend of self-will and relentlessness'.[2] First-century sources credit him with five serious infringements of the religious scruples of his subjects, three of which led to massacres, and a fourth nearly so.[3] The accounts depict a man who too readily took up a provocative stance, and having done so found it very hard to climb down. Caiaphas' delegation could not expect a sympathetic hearing.

[1] See above, p. 127.   [2] Philo, *Legatio ad Gaium* 38 (301).
[3] Lk. 13:1; Josephus, *Ant.* xviii. 3–4 (55–62; 85–89); Philo, *Legatio ad Gaium* 38 (299–305).

But they were well armed: no Roman governor could afford to ignore a charge of sedition, particularly a governor whom the Jewish authorities would have been only too pleased to denounce to Rome for failure to do his job.

Pilate, accordingly, received the delegation. The precise course of the hearing is not certain, but it is clear that Pilate was far from co-operative, and set himself to thwart the Jews' obvious intentions. It is only what we would expect of him, regardless of the judicial rights and wrongs of the case.

Luke tells us that an unexpected opportunity to drop the case presented itself quite early in the proceedings. In response to Pilate's stalling, the Jewish leaders started recounting Jesus' supposed revolutionary activity in Galilee; his Galilean origin was bound to tell against him on such a charge.[1] But if Jesus was a Galilean, he came from the tetrarchy of Herod Antipas, and Antipas was in Jerusalem for the Passover. Antipas, therefore, should hear the case.[2]

The 'hearing' before Antipas was a farce. Antipas had heard reports of Jesus' activities in Galilee, and of the impression he had made as a miracle-worker, so he was glad to have the chance to see the man for himself. But Jesus disappointed him: no miracles were forthcoming, and Jesus even refused to answer his questions. Denied any other entertainment in the encounter, Antipas joined his soldiers in making fun of the carpenter who called himself a king; but of any judicial proceedings we hear not a word. That was Pilate's job, and back to Pilate Jesus was sent.

---

[1] See above, p. 24, for the reputation of Galilee.

[2] The hearing before Antipas is recorded only by Luke (23:6–12), and is therefore sometimes suspected as a fabrication. But as it had no material effect on the course of the trial, there is no adequate reason for Luke to invent it, and it is not surprising that the other Gospels omit to mention it.

Sixth hearing: Pilate

So Pilate was obliged to handle the case.[1]

The charge, as all the Gospels agree, was political, focused on the title 'King of the Jews'. We have no record that Jesus ever used such a title, but it was an easy deduction from his Messianic claims for those who did not understand Messiahship as he did. Indeed his manner of arrival in Jerusalem virtually amounted to a claim to be the king expected in Zechariah 9:9. So Pilate asked him bluntly, 'Are you the king of the Jews?'

Faced with a direct challenge, as he had been before Caiaphas, Jesus for a second time broke his silence. But this time he was less definite: 'You say it.'[2] It is not a denial, but neither is it a straight acceptance. Jesus *is* king of the Jews, but not in the sense Pilate (and the Jewish leaders) are using the term. John tells us that Jesus went on to explain to Pilate that his kingship was 'not of this world'. And that was all he would say.

It was enough to convince Pilate that he was dealing with a trumped-up charge. This man was not a revolutionary, but a religious fanatic, eccentric perhaps, but not dangerous. To one with no religious axe to grind it must have been pretty obvious. Jesus' record, his bearing in the trial, and the over-eager concern of the Jewish religious leaders for the man's conviction, told their story plainly enough. Like one of his successors faced with a similar case, Pilate

[1] The outline of the trial that follows is based largely on the detailed account in Jn. 18:28 – 19:16. The other Gospels have much briefer accounts, though they agree on the essential points. John's account is a fine piece of dramatic narrative; C. H. Dodd, *Historical Tradition in the Fourth Gospel* (Cambridge, 1963), pp. 96–120, argues, nevertheless, that it is not the product of his imagination, but of a reliable tradition independent of the other Gospels.

[2] See above, p. 147, note 3. The same form of expression which is used in Mt. 26:64 here occurs in all three Synoptic Gospels.

decided to 'pronounce him a maniac and let him go'.[1]

An attractive way of accomplishing this was to invoke the established practice of releasing a Jewish prisoner as a conciliatory gesture at the Passover festival.[2] So Pilate offered to release Jesus as this year's amnesty. It was not a very clever idea, because the essence of the custom was the release of a *popular* prisoner, and Jesus was anything but popular with that section of the population to whom Pilate made the offer. The priests had their own candidate ready, Barabbas, a true popular hero. They had also apparently taken the precaution of gathering a big enough crowd to provide a convincing demonstration of popular support for their demands. Pilate's clumsy proposal was drowned in shouts of 'Barabbas'. And mingled with them was a growing chorus of demands that Jesus should be crucified.

Much is sometimes made of the fickleness of the Jerusalem crowd which could welcome Jesus with hosannas, and a few days later clamour for his death. But there is no reason to suppose they were the same people. It was the Passover pilgrims who welcomed Jesus, but what pilgrim worth his salt would be hanging around the governor's palace early on the morning of the great day of the festival, when there was so much to be prepared? Besides, the narrow street outside the 'praetorium', where the trial was held, would not allow a very large crowd to

[1] This was the verdict of Albinus, procurator of Judaea AD 62–64, when asked by the Jewish authorities to deal with another Jesus, son of Ananias, a persistent prophet of doom, who likewise refused to speak in his own defence (Josephus, *B.J.* vi. 5. 3 (300–309)).

[2] The practice is not otherwise attested (unless it is hinted at in Mishnah, *Pesaḥim* 8:6), though this is hardly surprising if it was a purely local concession, perhaps Pilate's own innovation to try to keep on the right side of his unpredictable subjects. There are a few records of similar amnesties in the Roman Empire, though none is quite parallel; but modern experience is sufficient to show the value of a popular amnesty as a political weapon.

gather, only a small fraction of the thousands in Jerusalem that weekend. It is hardly likely that the Jewish leaders, who had planned the arrest and trial of Jesus so carefully, left the composition of the crowd to chance: 'rent-a-crowd' is not a purely modern technique. There was still significant popular support for Jesus when he set out for execution;[1] meanwhile the vast majority of those who had welcomed him a few days earlier were too intent on their Passover preparations to realize that anything was happening.

The Roman verdict

Beaten in his attempt to discharge Jesus completely, Pilate tried a compromise. He sent the prisoner to be scourged. This was serious enough, for scourging was a regular prelude to crucifixion, and was administered only for capital or other very serious offences. The victim was tied to a post, and his back flayed raw with leather thongs. Often the scourging was itself fatal.

But Pilate does not seem yet to have intended it to be fatal. It was another attempt to thwart the Jewish demands by substituting a less than capital sentence. He seems to have relied on the popular demand for Jesus' blood being satisfied by this savage punishment. To add to the psychological effect, his soldiers mockingly dressed the wounded man in a royal robe, and put on his head a crown made of thorny twigs, for while Pilate was keen to deny the priests their victim, he had no love for religious impostors either. The result was a blend of savagery and ridicule which he reckoned was as humiliating as they could wish, and so he brought the pathetic figure out to the crowd: 'Look! Here is the man!'

Lk. 23:27.

But he had miscalculated. The Jewish punishment for blasphemy was death, and they would accept nothing less from the Romans. The shouts for his crucifixion only increased.

Yet still Pilate stalled. His reluctance to condemn Jesus to death is so marked in the Gospels that some have suspected that it is a propaganda device to impress Roman readers with Jesus' innocence, rather than historical fact. But it was quite in character for Pilate to want to thwart the Jewish leaders, even if not to stand up for justice. Quite independent confirmation comes from a Jewish tradition that Jesus could not be condemned out of hand 'because he was close to the government';[1] a memory of Pilate's reluctance to convict would account for this belief that Jesus enjoyed Roman favour.

C. H. Dodd graphically speaks of 'the unrelenting pressure which the priests exert, while the governor turns and doubles like a hunted hare'.[2] This pressure now reached its climax in a thinly veiled threat to report Pilate to his superiors for failure to deal with a clear case of treason: 'If you set him free that means you are not the Emperor's friend! Anyone who claims to be a king is the Emperor's enemy!' It was not an empty threat, for when Pilate was finally removed from office a few years later, it was in just this way, when his Samaritan subjects reported his mis-government to the governor of Syria, and Pilate was recalled to Rome to answer to the emperor.[3]

This time Pilate was effectively cornered. He could not afford to ignore political blackmail. After a few ineffectual protests, he signed the death-warrant, and Jesus was led away.

[1] Babylonian Talmud, *Sanhedrin* 43a.
[2] *Historical Tradition in the Fourth Gospel*, p. 97.
[3] Josephus, *Ant.* xviii. 4. 2 (88–89).

The crucifixion

It was not every day that the Roman guards had a self-proclaimed king at their mercy. Like the Jewish guards who had held Jesus during the night, they made the most of the occasion as they got ready to take him for execution. By the time Jesus stumbled out of the guard-room with the beam of the cross crushing his raw back, it is no wonder that people wept and wailed at the sight of him.[1]

Cicero described crucifixion as 'the most cruel and revolting punishment', and Josephus called it 'the most pitiable of deaths'. It was originally inflicted by the Romans only on slaves, but by the time of Jesus rebellious subjects in the provinces were executed this way as well; the gruesome sight of writhing and screaming rebels was supposed to be a good deterrent. It was not a punishment permitted by Jewish law, but Judaea under the Romans seems to have seen more than its fair share of crucifixions, often in large numbers at once.

The details of that inhuman execution are best left to the imagination; it is not likely to outrun the horrors of the fact. There is no reason to think that Jesus' crucifixion was different from any other, beyond the fact that of the two common methods of fastening the victim to the cross, ropes and nails, his was the more vicious. A stranger going by would see him hanging as a rebel among other rebels, a sight too often seen before and since, with the mocking label 'King of the Jews' to emphasize the folly of challenging the might of Rome.

But if the physical brutality was not out of the ordinary run of crucifixions, there was a marked difference in the victim himself. For one thing, he died very quickly: crucified men often lingered on in agony for two or three

[1] Lk. 23:27.

days, yet Jesus died within a few hours.[1] And while most victims, first maddened by the pain, gradually slipped into unconsciousness, Jesus, to judge from the reports of his words on the cross, remained fully conscious to the end. He refused the narcotic drink which was customarily provided by the good ladies of Jerusalem to numb the victims' senses;[2] it was his mission to suffer, and he accepted it with a clear mind. When he died, he died suddenly, as if by a deliberate act of will. The Gospel accounts suggest that in a sense it was Jesus, not the Roman guards or the jeering priests, who was in charge of the situation.

Most victims would curse and scream while they had the strength. Jesus died with a prayer.[3] And his few recorded words before that show more concern for others than for himself.[4] But one great cry in particular has impressed itself on the memory of Christian and non-Christian alike: 'My God, my God, why did you abandon me?'[5] They are the opening words of Psalm 22, and they give us a glimpse of what it really meant for Jesus to 'bear the sin of many'; the experience he had dreaded the previous night in Gethsemane had come, and the effect was shattering. But soon the horror passed, and as Jesus' strength finally ebbed away, he uttered the one triumphant word, 'Finished!'[6]

It was all so extraordinary that even the Roman officer in charge of the execution squad, who must have witnessed plenty of crucifixions, was impressed. 'Certainly he was a good man!', Luke reports him as saying, while Mark has,

[1] Speculations about the precise physical cause of death by crucifixion are many. An agreed solution is unlikely ever to be found, in the absence (inevitably!) of experimental evidence.
[2] Mk. 15:23. The custom is recorded in Babylonian Talmud, *Sanhedrin* 43a.
[3] Lk. 23:46.   [4] Lk. 23:34, 43; Jn. 19:26, 27.   [5] Mk 15:34.
[6] Jn. 19:30. The Greek word is best paraphrased by 'I have done it!' NEB and Jerusalem Bible render, 'It is accomplished!'

'This man was really the Son of God!' (though what exactly that phrase would mean to a Roman soldier is hard to say).[1]

Who killed Jesus?

In the official archives, no doubt, none of this was noted, and Jesus was entered as just another Jewish rebel, properly disposed of. The only nearly contemporary reference to Jesus' death by a Roman historian says simply that he 'had undergone the death penalty in the reign of Tiberius, by sentence of the procurator Pontius Pilatus',[2] which, as far as it goes, is perfectly true.

It has sometimes been argued that that is all there is to it: Jesus was a political trouble-maker, and was executed by the Romans as such; the idea that the real pressure for his death came from the Jewish leaders is Christian propaganda to make Christianity respectable in Roman eyes. Unfortunately for this theory, it falls foul not only of the mass of documentation in the Gospels for Jesus' constant conflict with the Jewish leaders, and of the earliest Christian tradition available,[3] but Jewish tradition as well accepts that it was the Jews who were responsible for Jesus' death. The Talmud presents the whole of Jesus' trial and death as a Jewish judicial procedure, with no mention of the Roman governor's part in passing the sentence,[4] while Josephus' account says that Pilate crucified Jesus 'on an indictment by the chief men among us'.[5] Similarly the anti-Christian Celsus in the late second century could introduce into his

[1] Mk. 15:39; Lk. 23:47. [2] Tacitus, *Annals* xv. 44.
[3] I Thessalonians 2:14, 15, probably the earliest writing in the New Testament. *Cf.* the constant refrain in the early Christian sermons reported in Acts 2:23, 36; 3:13–17; 7:52; 13:27, 28.
[4] *Sanhedrin* 43a.
[5] *Ant.* xviii. 3. 3 (64). This famous passage has certainly been adapted by Christian hands since it left Josephus' pen, but it is widely accepted that the detail quoted is original.

argument an imaginary Jew who assumed as a matter of common knowledge that it was the Jews who 'convicted him, condemned him, and declared that he should be punished'.[1] Unexpected and quite independent confirmation comes in a letter from an otherwise unknown Syrian sage, Mara bar Serapion, probably neither Jewish nor Christian, who talks about the Jews' folly in 'executing their wise king', as a result of which their nation was ruined and scattered; again no mention of a Roman part in the trial.[2]

All this supports the account in the Gospels that Pilate's verdict was given under Jewish pressure, and that it was the Jewish leaders who were primarily responsible for Jesus' death. And on that basis has been built the whole hideous history of Christian persecution of Jews which is still not extinct. It is irrational, of course, to blame later generations of Jews for what their ancestors did. Besides, as we have seen throughout this book, the opposition to Jesus did not come from the Jewish people as a whole, but from the leading minority. Even at the end, it was probably only a small hand-picked crowd which shouted, 'Crucify him!'

But irrational prejudices die hard. Perhaps it would kill them more quickly if Christians looked to their own origins, to the first followers of Jesus, who, confronted by the same generation, indeed by the very men who sent Jesus to his death, called not for vengeance but for repentance, and pleaded with Jesus' fellow-countrymen to reverse their leaders' mistake and accept the claims of Jesus. And can anyone imagine that he himself would have approved any other attitude?

[1] Quoted by Origen, *Contra Celsum* ii. 4, 5, 9.
[2] The letter, probably written in the late first century AD, is most easily consulted in F. F. Bruce, *Jesus and Christian Origins outside the New Testament* (Hodder, 1974), pp. 30, 31.

Indeed, Peter and the other disciples did not regard even the Jewish leaders as *ultimately* responsible. 'My brothers, I know that what you and your leaders did to Jesus was done because of your ignorance. God long ago announced by means of all the prophets that his Messiah had to suffer; and he made it come true in this way. Repent, then, and turn to God ...'[1] What drove Jesus to the cross was ultimately not Jewish hostility, but his God-given mission to suffer and die as 'a ransom for many'. To describe Jesus' death as the result of the interplay of political and ideological forces in a very volatile part of the Roman Empire, or even as an example of religious bigotry at its most callous, may be perfectly true, but misses the essential point which has made the cross a paradoxical symbol of hope to millions ever since. It was not a political accident which took Jesus there; it was the purpose of God.

So Jesus died, and was buried. A proper burial for a crucified man was uncommon enough, and it shows the support Jesus still enjoyed even in the more influential sector of Jerusalem society that it was a rich landowner, himself a member of the Sanhedrin, who obtained permission to give the body a decent burial, and provided a new rock-cut tomb on his own land for the purpose. A number of rock-cut tombs have been found in the area, often with niches for several bodies. One of these, with a large stone rolled across the entrance to keep out animals and thieves, was used for the body of Jesus. No-one can be sure now which one it was, if indeed it was any of the ones so far discovered. In any case, as the next chapter will show, it no longer matters very much!

[1] Acts 3:17, 18; *cf.* 2:23.

11 Vindication

When the first Christian missionary came to Athens he was understood to be preaching two new deities, Jesus and Anastasis. 'Anastasis' is the Greek for 'resurrection', and Paul's preaching concentrated so much on the resurrection of Jesus that they apparently mistook 'Resurrection' for the goddess he worshipped alongside Jesus.[1] In this overriding emphasis, Paul was in line with all the earliest Christian preachers: their constant theme was, 'God has raised him from the dead.'

When the Athenian philosophers understood what Paul meant by 'Anastasis', some made fun of such an irrational idea; but some wanted to know more, and a very few were convinced.

It is still much the same today. To many people the idea that Jesus' body actually left the grave and that he appeared alive to a number of his followers before mysteriously vanishing from the earth is too preposterous to merit more than a passing sneer. Others are intrigued, but non-committal. But still to many, as to Paul and his few converts at Athens, it is the one supremely important fact of history, the rock on which their faith is built.

[1] Acts 17:18.

It is sometimes suggested that the growth and continued existence of the Christian church is the greatest argument for the fact of the resurrection of Jesus. The first Christians would hardly have put a known falsehood at the centre of their preaching, and claimed to have a living experience of a man whom they knew to be dead and buried. That their message won so many converts and survived hostility and outright persecution to become the daily faith of millions is not easy to square with its being deliberate make-believe. If the story of Jesus had finished at the end of the last chapter, it is hard to understand how Christianity could have got off the ground at all.

But if it was not a deliberate lie, might it not have been a sincere illusion? There are many conflicting religious and ideological systems which inspire fanatical devotion and win converts; they cannot all be right. One which rests on so improbable a claim as the historical resurrection of a dead man must surely produce firmer evidence than the fact that millions have believed it, even to the extent of dying for that belief.

So we come inevitably to the question of historical evidence. And here the problem is that 'historical' means different things to different people. To most ordinary folk it means 'what actually happened', even if that happening was unique and inexplicable. But many historians argue that only that can be called 'historical' which falls within the space-time structure and the system of cause and effect which is the framework for our understanding of our world. To talk about a dead body coming to life is therefore to go outside the realm of the 'historical' altogether.

Now the interesting thing is that the New Testament evidence for the resurrection of Jesus fits the historian's demand remarkably well. The Gospels make no attempt to describe Jesus' actual coming back to life, still less to explain the biological and other factors involved. What they do record for us are the much more down-to-earth (and so 'historical' in this special sense) factors of the experiences of those who found his grave empty and claimed to have met him alive. The very understandable reactions of quite normal people to this unique situation are well within the bounds of the historian's proper area of enquiry, and here the Gospels provide ample material for study. So it is with this 'historical fringe' of the unique event of Jesus' resurrection that we must concern ourselves before we can dare to speculate on just what that event involved.[1]

The historical evidence in the Gospels focuses on two main facts: the empty tomb, and the various encounters with the risen Jesus.

The empty tomb

It is commonly stated that the Gospel accounts of the finding of the empty tomb are hopelessly contradictory, and so cannot provide any reliable guide to what actually happened. A few minutes comparing the four accounts will certainly reveal that they differ quite radically both in their over-all structure and in the details they record. But how far are they actually contradictory?

The following account of the discovery of the empty tomb is drawn from *all four* Gospels; each detail in it is not only compatible with but is actually explicit in *each* of the four accounts:

[1] On the historical evidence see further Sir Norman Anderson's booklet, *The Evidence for the Resurrection* (Inter-Varsity Press, 1950), and more fully his *A Lawyer among the Theologians* (Hodder, 1973), chapters 3–4. A detailed study of the question of the empty tomb is provided by E. L. Bode, *The First Easter Morning* (Biblical Institute Press, 1970). Michael Green, in *Man Alive!* (Inter-Varsity Press, 1967), combines a careful study of the evidence with a lively discussion of the significance of the resurrection.

On the first day of the week, very early, some women,[1] including Mary of Magdala, came to the tomb where Jesus had been buried. They found the stone rolled away from the entrance, but Jesus' body was not there. They were alarmed. They saw there an angel or angels[2] dressed in white clothes ('shining' according to Luke), who spoke to them. The women then went off and reported their experiences to the disciples of Jesus.[3]

This area of explicit agreement is far from negligible. It includes the whole story in a basic form. Moreover, other details recorded by one evangelist or another would fit into this outline without involving any contradiction with the others, *e.g.* the angel as the agent in removing the stone (Matthew), Peter's subsequent visit to the tomb without seeing Jesus, and his discovery of the grave-clothes still in place (Luke and John), and a meeting of the women with Jesus himself outside the tomb (Matthew and John).

Other details are apparently in conflict. Some of them are not very important (*e.g.* the number of women, the number of angels, and whether they were sitting or standing). Others are more troublesome. Why did the women come with spices to anoint the body (Mark and Luke) if it had already been anointed (John) and the tomb was sealed and guarded (Matthew)? Why was Mary surprised to meet

[1] John mentions only one explicitly, but the use of the plural 'we do not know' in 20:2 implies that others were present.
[2] Luke and John mention two, Matthew and Mark only one. In Luke they are first described as 'men in bright shining clothes' (24:4), but later as 'angels' (24:23); in Mark it is 'a young man dressed in white' (16:5), who is normally taken to be an angelic messenger, like the 'men' in Luke. It is interesting that even the account of the resurrection in the second-century 'Gospel of Peter', which is full of extra supernatural phenomena, still describes the (two) angels by Mark's word, 'young men'.
[3] The basic text of Mark's Gospel breaks off before this point, but their report is clearly presupposed in the 'young man's' command to tell Peter and the others (16:7).

Jesus (John) if the angels had already told her about his resurrection (Matthew, Mark and Luke)?

It is quite clear, then, that the Gospel writers were not trying to harmonize their accounts, and it looks as though the details of the story took second place to the task of conveying a vivid impression of an unforgettable experience. It would indeed be a real ground for suspicion if four supposedly independent accounts of so mind-bending an event were to turn out identical. Even a road-accident usually produces eye-witness accounts which are hard to reconcile on paper. It is, therefore, all the more impressive that all four accounts agree on the essential features of the story, however differently they may express them.

It is worth noticing, too, that the accounts are really very down-to-earth in tone, despite the astonishing fact which they imply. The women worry about how they will move the stone, and run away in a panic despite the reassuring message of the angels; Peter and the 'other disciple' race to the tomb, and Peter loses the race, but is the first to pluck up the courage to go inside; Mary thinks Jesus is the gardener, and the disciples write off the women's report as empty gossip. Compare all this with the second-century *Gospel of Peter*, with its loud voice from heaven, angels descending, the stone rolling away by itself, and a (talking) cross following Jesus (whose head reached above the heavens) out of the tomb, and it looks as if the four Gospels are remarkably free from the pious legends which the church soon began to weave.

One feature which no Jew would invent, and yet which is in all four Gospels, is that the first witnesses to the empty tomb were *women*. A woman's testimony was not admissible in Jewish law, and no-one could be expected to take their story seriously (as in fact the disciples refused to do, at first). The only conceivable reason for claiming that *women* found the tomb empty is that it was true.

There is, then, good historical reason, from these Christian sources, to believe that Jesus' tomb was found to be empty. Additional confirmation of this is the persistent tradition that the Jewish authorities spread a rumour that the disciples stole the body. This rumour is reported by Matthew,[1] and in more detail by Justin in the second century.[2] Unless there was in fact some such official propaganda, it is hard to see why Matthew devotes so much space to reporting the setting of an official guard over the tomb, and John's report that the grave-clothes were still there and undisturbed[3] is probably also designed to squash this rumour. If the body was still in the tomb, there would have been no need for the authorities to resort to such defensive propaganda.

Moreover, the first Christians could hardly have preached the resurrection in Jerusalem itself if the body was still there to be seen. Even if it were psychologically possible for them to preach that Jesus was alive, and to worship him as the conqueror of death, within yards of the place where they knew his bones were lying, it is inconceivable that no-one challenged the claim and produced the body. It seems to have been accepted by everyone that Jesus' tomb was in fact empty; where they differed was in how they explained it.[4]

[1] Mt. 28:11–15.
[2] Justin, *Dial.* 108, quoting what purports to be the official Jewish circular on the subject.
[3] Jn. 20:6, 7.
[4] The desperate suggestion that it was all a genuine mistake, in that the women went to the wrong tomb, cannot account for the fact that no-one in Jerusalem pointed out the mistake, when they had ample motive for doing so. Nor did the Jews ever put forward the preposterous suggestion which is still occasionally resuscitated, that Jesus did not really die on the cross, revived in the tomb, and escaped. Even if this were physically possible, it makes the Christian belief in his *victory over death* even more difficult to explain: a mutilated invalid could hardly produce this effect. Advocates of this theory can know little about Roman crucifixion.

Geza Vermes, the Jewish historian, who certainly has no axe to grind in favour of Christian belief, concludes that 'in the end, when every argument has been considered and weighed, the only conclusion acceptable to the historian must be that the opinions of the orthodox, the liberal sympathizer and the critical agnostic alike – and even perhaps of the disciples themselves – are simply interpretations of the one disconcerting fact: namely that the women who set out to pay their last respects to Jesus found to their consternation, not a body, but an empty tomb.'[1]

Encounters with the risen Jesus

Striking as the fact of the empty tomb certainly is, it is remarkable that the rest of the New Testament nowhere specifically mentions it. It is interested not in the discarded cocoon, but in the new life which has emerged from it, the risen Christ. Thus when Paul sets out the grounds for Christian preaching of the resurrection,[2] while the empty tomb is certainly implied,[3] all the evidence marshalled consists of details of those who met Jesus alive after his crucifixion.

Luke says that 'for forty days after his death he showed himself to them (his disciples) many times, in ways that proved beyond doubt that he was alive'.[4] At least eleven such appearances are individually recorded,[5] some to

---

[1] *Jesus the Jew*, p. 41.   [2] 1 Corinthians 15:3–11.
[3] He mentions Jesus' death, burial and resurrection in close sequence (verses 3–4). It would have been meaningless to a Jew to speak of the 'resurrection' of one who lay dead in a tomb if the body was still there.
[4] Acts 1:3.
[5] Mt. 28:9–10, 16–20; Lk. 24:13–31, 36–49 (= Jn. 20: 19–23; 1 Corinthians 15:5 'all twelve apostles'?); Jn. 20:11–18, 24–29; 21: 1–14; Acts 1:6–9 (= 1 Corinthians 15:7 'all the apostles'?); 1 Corinthians 15:5 (Peter: = Lk. 24:34); 1 Corinthians 15:6 (500 followers); 1 Corinthians 15:7 (James). Paul also includes his own encounter with the risen Christ in the list (1 Corinthians 15:8), but this falls well outside the immediate post-resurrection period.

single individuals (Mary of Magdala, Peter, James), others to small groups (the two on the Emmaus road, the Twelve, the Galilee fishermen), and one to a staggering five hundred disciples at once, most of whom Paul can claim are still alive to vouch for the truth of his report.[1]

Some of these encounters are reported to have been in and around Jerusalem, just after the resurrection (so Matthew, Luke and John), others in Galilee (Matthew and John), and the sequence finished, according to Luke, back in Jerusalem a few days before Pentecost, some six weeks after the resurrection. Probably the disciples returned home to Galilee after the Passover with other pilgrims, and came back to Jerusalem for Pentecost; this was what was expected of a good Jew, though not all were so scrupulous about the lesser festivals.

The risen Jesus was apparently able to meet them wherever they were. There is no suggestion that he travelled or lived with them; the recorded appearances are all relatively brief encounters in a single place, usually beginning and ending suddenly or mysteriously. Jesus 'drew near', was seen standing in the garden or on the shore, 'stood among them' in a room with the doors locked, 'disappeared from their sight' in the middle of a meal. The impression given is not of a simple return to the normal conditions of life, but of a new mode of existence, free from the physical limitations of space and time.

Yet the Gospel writers are at pains to stress that the risen Jesus was no mere ghost. He appeared in broad daylight, and took his place in everyday situations, a journey, a meal, a fishing trip. He looked so ordinary that Mary mistook him for a gardener, and the disciples on the Emmaus road accepted him without question as a fellow-traveller. He could break bread, serve breakfast, and eat

[1] I Corinthians 15:6.

food. He could invite the sceptical Thomas to feel the crucifixion scars in his hands and side. These are not the characteristics of ghosts, visions or hallucinations. All the accounts agree in presenting the risen Jesus as a real, if unique, physical person.

To attempt a more exact analysis of the make-up of Jesus' resurrection body would be futile. We have no other data. But such as we have tell us that his body left the grave, leaving no remainder, solidly physical and still recognizably Jesus, and yet transformed so as to be free from the limitations of time and space. Such at least, by their own account, is how his followers encountered him.

It is sometimes suggested that these supposed encounters were really hallucinations, suggested to the excited and exhausted minds of the disciples by long-cherished hopes that Jesus could never die. It would be a neat theory if it did not fall foul of all the facts! It would be hard indeed to find another example of hallucinations of so unvarying a form which were experienced by a wide range of characters (some far from suggestible, such as Thomas), sometimes alone, sometimes in quite large groups, frequently over a concentrated period, after which they abruptly stopped. But the fatal flaw in this explanation is that a bodily resurrection is the last thing they expected. The women's report was dismissed as empty gossip, and Thomas would not believe even the united testimony of his closest colleagues. It never occurred to Mary of Magdala or to the disciples on the Emmaus road who he was until he himself prompted them. It is quite true that Jesus had taught them that he would rise again, but the Gospels tell us they had not understood[1] – hardly surprisingly, since Jewish thought had no room for the bodily resurrection of an individual before the last day. No doubt they

[1] Jn. 20:9; cf. Mk. 9:9, 10, 31, 32; Lk. 18:33, 34.

thought he was talking metaphorically about a spiritual vindication[1] until facts proved that he meant it literally.

This, then, is the focus of the historical evidence for the resurrection of Jesus offered by the New Testament, the testimony of a large number of his disciples that, quite contrary to their expectations, they met him after his crucifixion and burial, not just resuscitated but triumphantly raised to a new and glorious life. Taken with the compelling evidence for the empty tomb, it goes about as far as historical evidence could possibly go towards proving the bodily resurrection of Jesus. No other plausible explanation of the facts has yet been offered.

The implications of the evidence

But when the historian has done his work, the debate is not ended. For the historical evidence points to a conclusion for which there is no 'historical' (in the narrow sense) explanation. Where historical evidence demands a supernatural explanation, we are faced with a difficult choice, one which has already confronted us over the miracles of Jesus, and over his miraculous birth.[2] It is the basic choice which divides the man of faith from the secular mind.

You may refuse to allow that anything can happen which our present knowledge of the world cannot explain, at least in principle, in terms of natural science. You are then committed to the apparently unscientific course of rejecting the conclusion to which the evidence clearly points, without even the consolation of a plausible alternative explanation. Resurrection of a dead man is impossible, therefore it did not happen. What did happen to give rise to the facts of the empty tomb and the encounters with the risen Jesus must

[1] *Cf.* Hosea 6:2 for the same language used in this sense.
[2] See above, pp. 73-76, 32-34.

be left unanswered: the only adequate answer has been ruled out *a priori*.

Or you may take the apparently more scientific course of following the evidence where it leads. But then you must give up the security of a tidily comprehensible view of the world as a closed system of natural law. You have to admit that man is not the measure of all things. And once you allow the resurrection of Jesus as a fact, where do you stop? There is no good reason then for refusing to allow at least the possibility of miracles, and of a virgin birth. In fact, you will find that you have let God into the world, and that is more than many men can face up to. It is undeniably more comfortable, if less scientific, to refuse to follow the evidence where it leads.

Jesus constantly confronts us with this choice, most inescapably in his resurrection, but also to varying degrees throughout his life. His whole life presupposes the reality of God, as an active force in the world he has made. Jesus and a secular world-view do not mix.

That is why, for all the evidence, there have always been many who refused to believe that Jesus rose from the dead, from the philosophers of Athens to the secular thinkers of today. It is not that the evidence is inadequate: it could hardly be better. It is simply that for some people no evidence could ever be enough to justify the radical rethink of their whole world-view which Jesus demands.

Christ triumphant

So the story of Jesus comes to its climax in a frankly supernatural event, yet told in a quite natural, matter-of-fact way. It is a fitting end to a story which has been throughout a fascinating mixture of miracle and down-to-earth humanity, of supernatural occurrences in a setting of everyday life, of God at work among men.

It closes with Jesus, the crucified heretic, triumphantly vindicated, 'shown with great power to be the Son of God, by being raised from death.'[1] The victim has become the victor. The prophecy of Daniel 7:13, 14 which he had so often quoted is now gloriously fulfilled: 'I have been given all authority in heaven and on earth. Go, then, to all peoples everywhere and make them my disciples.'[2] This was the conviction which sent Peter and his colleagues boldly out into the streets of Jerusalem, calling men to repent and 'know for sure that it is this Jesus, whom you nailed to the cross, that God has made Lord and Messiah'.[3]

All the Gospels end with Jesus risen, triumphant, vindicated. In Matthew's Gospel he promises his followers, 'I will be with you always, to the end of the age.'[4] In John he says he is going back to the Father, and gives them the Holy Spirit to be with them in his place.[5] But Luke records how these promises took visible form when, some six weeks after his resurrection, Jesus took the disciples on to the Mount of Olives and there, after giving them his final instructions, disappeared into a cloud.[6] It was a vivid way of conveying to them that they could not expect his visible presence any longer, that he was not going to linger on earth, and eventually die and be forgotten. As he had warned his judges, the helpless prisoner in the dock was now to be 'seated at the right hand of the Almighty'.[7] It was thus, in the place of highest honour and authority, that his followers were to envisage him from now on, no longer limited by time and space, but dynamically present with them, always, everywhere.

[1] Romans 1:4.   [2] Mt. 28:18, 19.   [3] Acts 2:36.
[4] Mt. 28:20.
[5] Jn. 20:17, 22; cf. the constant emphasis in chapters 14–16.
[6] Acts 1:4–11; cf. Lk. 24:50, 51.
[7] Mk. 14:62, alluding to Psalm 110:1, which soon became one of the most-quoted Old Testament passages among the first-century Christians.

So, in the triumphant experiences of the days between Passover and Pentecost, began the movement which eventually brought Paul to Athens with his intriguing message of Jesus and Anastasis.

12 Dilemma

Jesus often made people uncomfortable, for he confronted them with a choice they would rather not have made.

A typical occasion was when he was asked to heal a cripple.[1] To everyone's surprise, he declared instead, 'My son, your sins are forgiven.' It was not only apparently irrelevant; it was practically blasphemous, as some of the scribes immediately realized, because only God could forgive sins. But Jesus was unrepentant. 'I will prove to you, then, that the Son of Man has authority on earth to forgive sins', he said, and did so by healing the man with a word. It left the scribes a difficult choice: either he was an impostor, in which case they had to explain away his miraculous cure, or he wielded an authority which by common consent was God's sole prerogative. They would rather not have had to decide.

The authority of Jesus
It was this calm assumption of authority which made Jesus so conspicuous, and so uncomfortable. Both his words and his deeds, the Gospels tell us, impressed the crowds above all with his authority.[2] It was not that he

[1]Mk. 2:1–12.   [2]Mk. 1:22, 27; Mt. 9:8.

went out of his way to *claim* authority; indeed he even refused to argue the matter when his authority was challenged.[1] But it was there, all the more unmistakable because it was so coolly taken for granted.

We have seen how his cures of both physical and spiritual illness by a simple word of command must have contrasted with the rigmarole of the professional Jewish healers and exorcists, and how they reminded the Roman officer of his own uncomplicated acceptance of the authority of a military order. 'Just say the word, and my servant will get well.'[2]

It was even more obvious when they listened to his teaching. Naturally enough, his fellow-townsmen at Nazareth could not fathom it: 'When they heard him they were all amazed. "Where did he get all this?" they asked. "What wisdom is this that has been given him?"'[3] Any other Jewish teacher made very sure that his teaching was documented with extensive quotations from Scripture and with the names of his teachers added to give weight to his opinion; his authority must always be second-hand. But not Jesus. He simply laid down the law. One of his favourite expressions to introduce a particularly weighty utterance was, 'Amen, I say to you, ...' Not 'Scripture says', or 'Rabbi X said', but 'I say'. Even the Old Testament prophets, with their conviction of receiving the word of the Lord direct, would only claim 'Thus says the Lord'. But Jesus spoke in his own name, and authenticated it with the solemn 'Amen' ('sure', 'reliable'), which no other teacher ever dared to use for his own words. No wonder they were astonished, at times even shocked.

It was the same cool assumption of authority which carried all before him when Jesus waded, single-handed, into the commercial bustle of the Court of the Gentiles,

[1] Mk. 11:27-33.   [2] See above, pp. 67-72.   [3] Mk. 6:2.

and cleared it at a stroke. There was, apparently, something irresistible about the impact of Jesus.

Perhaps the most remarkable proof of this authority is the fact that hard-headed men were prepared to leave their homes and livelihood, to accept impossibly exacting demands, with the promise of hardship, unpopularity, and outright persecution, and for what? For the mere 'Follow me' of a man whose mission they only dimly understood, but whom it was impossible for them to refuse. The wonder is not that some found the pace too hot, but that any stuck with him at all. But they did, and they still do. Once you have met Jesus, it is hard to shrug him off.

Who was Jesus?

Undeniably, then, there was something impressive and compelling about Jesus. He certainly had a generous endowment of that elusive human quality called 'leadership'. If he had wanted to lead an army, he would have made a great general. But that is not enough to explain the authority with which he acted and taught, despite his lack of all the expected qualifications for leadership.

One remarkable feature of Jesus' teaching as the Gospels record it is how much he talks about himself, and what staggering claims these sayings involve. He called men to believe in *him*, to trust *him*, he demanded their uncompromising allegiance to *himself*, and declared that the criterion of their final judgment would be their response to *him*. *He* sent them out, in *his* name; *he* gave them power and protection, *he* forgave sins, and invited the distressed, 'Come to *me*, and *I* will give you rest.'[1] In one remarkable passage he pictured himself as judge of all nations, sitting

[1] This feature is well known in John's Gospel, particularly in the 'I am' sayings. But the above examples are all drawn from the Synoptic Gospels. For a fuller account see A. M. Hunter, *The Work and Words of Jesus* (SCM Press, 1950), pp. 87–90.

as king on his throne, and pronouncing eternal judgment on the basis of what men had done to *him*.[1] All this (and there is much more like it) suggests that his authority rested not only on a commanding personality, still less on the skill of a successful demagogue, but on the claim to a unique status.

There is a paradox here, for this is the same Jesus who taught the need for humility and unselfishness, and gave an example of it by washing his disciples' feet. Often he went out of his way to avoid the attentions of a crowd excited by his miracles, and his reluctance to make an open declaration of his Messiahship teased both his supporters and his enemies. He repeatedly insisted that all his authority came from God, without whom he could do nothing, and the hours he spent in prayer showed that he meant what he said.

Yet all the time there is the assumption, which some-times comes to the surface, of a unique relationship with God, which is the real basis of his authority. Most remark-able is the way he regularly referred to God as his Father, and addressed him in prayer by the familiar Aramaic term 'Abba', the child's address to his father. No other Jew had ever dared to approach God like that. It is true that he taught his disciples to trust God as their Father, and to pray to him as such, but it is a striking fact that he never once coupled himself with them as sons of God in the same sense. The only time he said 'Our Father' was when he was teaching them what *they* should say; he did not say it with them. He was God's son in a unique sense.

He spelt it out like this: 'My Father has given me all things. No one knows the Son except the Father, and no one knows the Father except the Son, and those to whom

[1] Mt. 25:31–46.

the Son wants to reveal him.'[1] John tells us that the Jewish leaders were not slow to grasp the implications of this sort of language, and decided to kill him because in this way he made himself equal with God.[2] If it did not often come to the surface, the implication was constantly there, that Jesus' relationship with God was more than that of a worshipper, however devout, with the deity; it was the family relationship of one divine being with another, of the only Son with his Father.[3]

The call for decision

Claims like that drive men to extremes. Either you accept his authority as tantamount to that of God himself, which is what his disciples seem to have done; or you declare the man a dangerous impostor, and determine to destroy him, as most of the establishment did. But, once you have grasped the nature of his claims, it is difficult to be neutral. Eduard Schweizer puts it even more strongly: 'Neutrality is in any case impossible as a definitive attitude, for his summons is such that whoever seeks to remain neutral has already rejected him.'[4]

This is the dilemma with which Jesus confronted the men of his day, and with which he still confronts those who take the trouble to understand what his mission was all about. And still today, as then, it divides men deeply from one another.

It has always been a minority who have responded positively. In Jesus' own story of the sower and the seed, it

[1] Mt. 11:27. Again there are many similar sayings, particularly in John, *e.g.* 10:30; 14:6–10; 17:2–5.
[2] See Jn. 5:18.
[3] A full discussion of the nature of Jesus as human and divine is outside the scope of this book. The question is helpfully treated by L. Morris, *The Lord from Heaven* (second ed., Inter-Varsity Press, 1974).
[4] *Jesus* (SCM Press, 1971), p. 6.

was only a fraction of the seed which fell on fertile ground and produced a crop: the rest either failed to penetrate at all, or did not go deep enough to survive, or was choked by other more natural growths. It has always been like that.

It would be much more convenient if Jesus could be made to fit the formulas which we are all so good at devising for him, as the ethical reformer, the pacifist, the prophet of the oppressed classes, or whatever. All of these he is, and much more. But he cannot be reduced to any one of them. The only meaningful way to relate to the Jesus of the Gospels is in the totality of the claims he makes on us. If we do not come to him on his terms, we do not come to *him* at all.

The Jesus of the Gospels presents himself to us as the only hope of man in his estrangement from God, the one who by his death 'as a ransom for many' has made it possible for men to find a place in the true people of God, the community of the forgiven. He presents himself to all men, whatever their race or class. He does not demand that they subscribe to a particular theological system, but that they come to *him*, in that unreserved commitment which irrevocably changes the direction of a man's life and sets him apart from those who live only for what this world has to offer. That is what the New Testament means by 'faith', and it is in faith that a man comes to Jesus, or not at all.

So Jesus still demands decision, and demands it urgently, as urgently as the treasure hidden in the field which calls for a drastic renunciation of all other possessions if it is to be bought up before anyone else stumbles on it.[1] Jesus does not pretend that the decision will be easy: 'Go in through the narrow gate, for the gate is wide and the road is easy that leads to hell, and there are many who travel it.

[1] Mt. 13:44; *cf.* the simile of the pearl in verses 45, 46.

The gate is narrow and the way is hard that leads to life, and few people find it.'[1]

But it is not to be shrugged off because it is hard, for the results of evasion are serious:

'Everyone who hears these words of mine and obeys them will be like a wise man who built his house on the rock. The rain poured down, the rivers flooded over, and the winds blew hard against that house. But it did not fall, because it had been built on the rock.

Everyone who hears these words of mine and does not obey them will be like a foolish man who built his house on the sand. The rain poured down, the rivers flooded over, the winds blew hard against that house, and it fell.

What a terrible fall that was!'[2]

[1] Mt. 7:13, 14.   Mt 7:24–27.

Appendix

The Gospels as sources for a study of Jesus

Throughout this book I have drawn freely on the Gospels on the understanding that they are a legitimate source of information about Jesus. I have said very little about the character of the information they offer, or about the question of their reliability as historical sources.

Many readers will be quite content that it should be so; they have no difficulty in taking the Gospels more or less at their face-value as accounts of the historical figure, Jesus of Nazareth. It is for their sake that I have kept until the end what logically, perhaps, should have come at the beginning. For them it would have been an unnecessary distraction to be faced at the outset with a discussion of the character and status of the Gospels as historical sources; it might even have stopped them reading any further. They may well feel that they can ignore this appendix without loss – and they may well be right.

But others are aware that not everyone has so optimistic a view of the reliability of the Gospels. At least they will realize that a book such as this cannot be written without making some quite fundamental assumptions about the Gospels, and they will quite fairly expect to see those assumptions declared and defended. It is for them that this appendix is written; not of course to set out a fully documented defence of my understanding of the nature of the Gospels (that would take a book considerably longer than this one), but at least to declare my stance, and to give some indication of the reasons for it.

Sources outside the Gospels

It may sometimes be a cause of suspicion that Christian writers about Jesus draw their material almost exclusively from the Gospels, which have admittedly a clear Christian bias. In fact they may fairly be described as propaganda. Surely, therefore, any fair treatment ought to look for more objective sources.

The problem is that there are none! There is, of course, plenty of material which will give us a picture of the world in which Jesus lived, and I have tried to make good use of such material. But for information on Jesus himself there is pitifully little from non-Christian sources deriving from anywhere near the relevant period; practically all that has any claim to historical value has in fact been referred to in this book, and the reader could be forgiven for failing to notice its presence at all, there is so little of it.[1]

Tacitus mentions Jesus' execution by order of Pilate.[2] Josephus, in so far as the original form of his reference to Jesus can be reconstructed,[3] probably confirms his execution by crucifixion under Pilate (at Jewish instigation) and mentions his reputation as a miracle-worker and teacher. Jewish traditions preserved in the Talmud tell us that Jesus was executed by the Jewish leaders on Passover

---

[1] For full details of the sources, Christian and non-Christian, other than the New Testament see F. F. Bruce, *Jesus and Christian Origins outside the New Testament* (Hodder, 1974).
[2] See above, p. 157.
[3] *Ant.* xviii. 3. 3 (64). See above, p. 157.

Eve, primarily as a sorcerer and deceiver;[1] other possible references to Jesus in the Talmud add nothing of substance. The letter of the Syrian Mara bar Serapion[2] also refers to the Jews' execution of 'their wise king' at some time before the destruction of Jerusalem in AD 70. And that is that, as far as non-Christian sources go, until anti-Christian polemic was crystallized into the Jewish *Toledoth Jesu* in the Middle Ages, and various Jewish and Christian traditions found their way, sometimes in scarcely recognizable forms, into the Qur'an and other Islamic writings.[3]

So from non-Christian sources we could know for certain that Jesus lived and taught in Palestine, attained fame as a miracle-worker, and was crucified by the Roman authorities (at Jewish instigation) in the late twenties or early thirties of the first century AD. And that is all. But then we may well ask what further impact an itinerant preacher in a remote province of the Empire might be expected to make on the secular history of the period. It was hardly the sort of movement to hit the Roman headlines.

Christian sources outside the New Testament have little to offer either. For the most part the 'Gospels' produced during the second century and later are clearly based on the four canonical Gospels, reinforced by a steadily-growing accumulation of legendary material. The only document with any serious claim to preserve any independent traditions of Jesus is the *Gospel of Thomas*, a collection of 114 sayings attributed to Jesus, some of which are very close to those in the canonical Gospels, but several clearly reflect the move towards Gnostic thought which dominates much second-century Christian

[1] Babylonian Talmud, *Sanhedrin* 43a.
[2] See above, p. 158.
[3] Early references to Christians occur in Suetonius (*Claudius* 25. 4; *Nero* 16. 2) and in Pliny's correspondence with Trajan (*Epistles* x. 96–97), but neither tells us anything about Jesus himself.

writing. The only sound historical method is to use the contents of the admittedly primary sources (the canonical Gospels) to control our estimate of the later, derivative accounts. If this method eliminates the odd saying of Jesus here and there which might be genuine, it is hardly likely to affect our portrait of Jesus significantly. On this basis we may safely leave the later 'Gospels' out of account for the purposes of this book.

So for details of the life and teaching of Jesus, indeed for everything beyond the bare fact that he lived, died, and gave rise to a world religion, we are thrown back on the four Gospels. But can we trust them?[1] Are they not hopelessly biased, concerned only to project an image of Jesus as early Christian faith conceived him, not to give an objective historical assessment of the man as he really was?

The Gospels as history

'It seems to be an extremely tenaciously-held misapprehension among exegetes,' comments one scholar, 'that an early Christian author must *either* be a purposeful theologian and writer *or* a fairly reliable historian.'[2] This is a fair comment on the curious fact that different standards often seem to be demanded of the biblical writers than historians expect in other areas. It is generally accepted that few, if any, historians write without a bias. Many of the greatest histories were written with a clear axe to grind, but they are not therefore dismissed as of no value in reconstructing the actual course of events. There is no *a priori* reason why a writer with a message need necessarily misrepresent the facts to get his message across. Only if

[1] A useful guide to this subject, concerning the New Testament as a whole, is F. F. Bruce, *The New Testament Documents: Are They Reliable?* (fifth ed., Inter-Varsity Press, 1960).
[2] B. Gerhardsson, *Memory and Manuscript* (Uppsala, 1961), p. 209.

he can be shown to be guilty of actual distortion is there fair ground for rejecting his account. It is a basic legal principle that one is presumed innocent until proved to be guilty, but critics of the biblical writers sometimes seem to regard themselves as exempt from this requirement!

One reason for this apparently arbitrary scepticism about the reliability of the Gospels as history is not so much a historical as a philosophical one. The Gospels are full of miracles, and miracles do not happen; therefore the Gospels must be suspect. No scholar would put it so crudely, of course, but undoubtedly a disinclination to accept the reality of the supernatural is a powerful incentive to finding reasons for rejecting the Gospels as history.[1]

But the only fair way of judging a writer's performance would seem to be to look at what he himself says about his aims and method, and to check as far as possible by outside data how far his work measures up to his stated purpose.

One of the Gospel writers gives us a good opportunity for such a test. Luke prefaces his Gospel by a clear statement of intent. He plans to write an orderly account of the events that have occurred, based on careful study of the reports of eye-witnesses and of many previous writers on the subject, so as to bring out 'the full truth of all those matters which you have been taught'.[2] If words mean anything, Luke is very much concerned for sheer factual accuracy, and has taken great pains to achieve it.

Now it happens that in the case of Luke we are also in an unusually good position to check his performance against the witness of outside sources, for the second volume of his work, the Acts of the Apostles, involves numerous incidental references to persons, events and

[1] See above, pp. 32–34, 73–76, 169, 170, on the miraculous element in the Gospels.
[2] Lk. 1:1–4.

institutions of the Mediterranean world of the mid-first-century, and the accuracy of these references, even to quite obscure local officials, has been common knowledge since an extensive study of the subject led Sir William Ramsay to a radical change of mind about Luke, from a sceptical reserve to warm praise of his historical judgment and reliability. More recently attention has focused primarily on Luke's theological interests, but Ramsay's conclusions on his historical integrity have not been overthrown.[1]

Yet it is this Luke, with his care for factual accuracy, who has recorded for us far more miracles and supernatural experiences than any other New Testament writer. This fact, embarrassing as it is to our 'modern' view of history, suggests that for him the careful writing of history included the recording of supernatural events as a matter of course, not as edifying fiction, but because they happened. It is only if your philosophy rules out the supernatural that you have reason to doubt the reliability of Luke as a historian.

The other Gospel writers do not set out their programme so clearly as Luke, nor is there the same opportunity to check their performance against outside sources. What is clear, however, at least in the cases of Matthew and Mark, is that they are writing the same kind of book as Luke, with a purpose and method the more obviously similar to his when their writings are compared with any other class of ancient literature.

John's Gospel is different in character, and until fairly recently it was fashionable to regard it as superb theology with a very flimsy basis in historical fact. That approach

[1] The literature is vast. It is well surveyed and discussed by I. H. Marshall, *Luke: Historian and Theologian* (Paternoster Press, 1970), pp. 53–76.

received a severe knock with the publication in 1963 of C. H. Dodd's *Historical Tradition in the Fourth Gospel*. Not that Dodd regards every word as plain unadorned 'history', but he has shown clearly that 'behind the Fourth Gospel lies an ancient tradition independent of the other Gospels, and meriting serious consideration as a contribution to our knowledge of the historical facts concerning Jesus Christ'.[1] Nowadays, John's Gospel is treated with greater respect as an account of the life and teaching of Jesus, as well as an incomparable theological account of his significance.

The sayings of Jesus

But if there are good grounds for taking seriously the factual element in the Gospels' account of Jesus, can a similar reliance be placed on their record of his *teaching*? For here again the assumption is very commonly made that the early Christians saw no harm in attributing to Jesus sayings which he never in fact uttered, but which expressed their understanding of what he would have said, with the result that the Gospels give us information not about what *Jesus* taught, but about what the early Christians believed about him.

I have discussed this question at some length elsewhere.[2] Here I can only state the conclusion of that discussion, that there is remarkably little evidence for the large-scale invention of 'sayings of Jesus' in the first few decades after the resurrection which many critics assume, and that there is in fact considerable indication in the New Testament that the sayings of Jesus were accorded a special respect as such. This is what might reasonably be expected in the

[1] *Op. cit.* (Cambridge, 1963), p. 423.
[2] 'The Authenticity of the Sayings of Jesus' in C. Brown (ed.), *History, Criticism and Faith* (Inter-Varsity Press, 1976).

setting of first-century Palestine, where there was among Jewish scholars a quite stringent demand for accuracy in the preservation of authoritative teaching, and it seems that in the Christian community the apostles in particular had a special role to play in the careful preservation of the tradition of Jesus' teaching. Moreover, scholars who have studied in detail the linguistic and stylistic features of the sayings of Jesus in the Gospels have been impressed by the distinctive teaching style which still runs through them despite years of oral transmission and translation into Greek.

This is not to suggest, of course, that Jesus' sayings were incorporated absolutely *verbatim* in the Gospels. Jesus most probably spoke in Aramaic, so that the sayings have at least undergone translation into Greek. Clearly, too, there has been a process of selection of the sayings which were preserved and incorporated into the Gospels, and in the process individual sayings were sometimes rearranged into suitable groups for teaching purposes. Comparison of the Gospels shows, too, that the exact wording of a saying may vary, in order to bring out the emphasis most appropriate to the individual writer's context. Sometimes, particularly in the Gospel of John, it may be quite a free paraphrase. But all this is a very different matter from *inventing* 'sayings of Jesus' to suit the needs of later decades, and the evidence suggests that such a practice is improbable. While there was room for some variation in the wording and order of the sayings preserved, we have every reason to rely on the *content* of the teaching of Jesus as recorded in the Gospels.

The Gospels as biographies of Jesus

I have assumed, then, in writing this book, that the Gospels writers did intend to tell their readers facts about the actual life and teaching of Jesus, not just about what later Christians believed about him, and that a fund of carefully preserved tradition, both written and oral, was available to them for this purpose. I find it frankly incredible that a community whose faith focused so exclusively on a single historical individual could have been as blithely unconcerned about the historical facts of his life and teaching as many modern scholars assume. It would be hard to find any historical parallel to such an attitude. Even if the Christian leaders and teachers themselves could have been content to let the historical basis of their faith slip away, surely their converts must have wanted to know more about the man they were committing themselves to (which is precisely what Luke 1:1–4 seems to suggest), and those to whom they preached, whether hostile or just uncommitted, could be expected to enquire about, and challenge, the historical basis of this new religion. A Christian church without a genuinely historical interest in the life and teaching of Jesus is hard to imagine, and it is even harder to explain its missionary success.

This is not to suggest, however, that the Gospels are simple objective biographies of Jesus. Far from it. They are preaching, teaching documents, propaganda even. They are written by committed men to bring others to the same commitment. The way the facts are related and the teaching selected is angled to this end, to show the unique significance of Jesus. To that extent they are biased. But then so is practically any worth-while biography: people do not write biographies from a clinical interest in mere facts, but because they believe the person is worth writing about, and they want to show why. This is no reason to dispute the facts they relate – indeed, it is a powerful incentive for them to get the facts right.

One way in which the Gospels do differ significantly

from what we today understand by 'biography' is obvious at first glance. The vast majority of Jesus' life is passed over in silence. His birth is mentioned in only two of the Gospels, and his childhood, education, employment, in fact everything up to about the age of thirty, is totally ignored apart from one story in Luke about his escapade at the age of twelve. Then the next three years or so, probably, occupies the whole of each Gospel, with a quite disproportionate amount of space devoted to the last week of his life. Clearly they were not aiming to tell his whole life-story, but only those aspects of his life which served their purpose of explaining his significance. Long chronological gaps did not worry them. Indeed chronology took second place altogether to the teaching aim of the Gospels, if we may judge from the fact that the same incidents sometimes seem to occur in a different order in different Gospels. Chronological order sometimes gives way to an effective logical sequence of teaching, or even of events. This is why no-one can be sure of the exact length of Jesus' ministry:[1] none of the Gospels troubles to spell out the chronology in detail. It is the events and sayings themselves which are of prime importance, not the drawing up of a *curriculum vitae* with exact dates and periods.

It is this characteristic of the Gospels which has dictated the structure of this book. It would have been very satisfying to write a modern-style 'biography' of Jesus, setting out all the events of his life in chronological order. But the Gospels do not do that, and they are our only detailed sources. So we must follow where they lead. Where they provide a clear and consistent chronological framework (*i.e.* in the narratives of Jesus' birth, the opening of his ministry, and the last week of his life) I have written chronologically, but for the period of Jesus' ministry as a

[1] See above, p. 45.

whole I have used a thematic rather than a chronological framework, because it was clearly the main themes, rather than the chronology, of Jesus' life and teaching which were the chief concern of the Gospel writers.[1]

See above, p. 48, for some remarks on the likely chronological development of the ministry of Jesus.